# DOING BUSINESS IN CHINA

OTHER ECONOMIST BOOKS

Guide to Analysing Companies
Guide to Business Modelling
Guide to Business Planning
Guide to Economic Indicators
Guide to the European Union
Guide to Financial Management
Guide to Financial Markets
Guide to Hedge Funds
Guide to Investment Strategy
Guide to Management Ideas and Gurus
Guide to Organisation Design
Guide to Project Management
Guide to Supply Chain Management
Numbers Guide
Style Guide

Book of Obituaries
Brands and Branding
Business Consulting
Buying Professional Services
The City
Coaching and Mentoring
Dealing with Financial Risk
Economics
Emerging Markets
The Future of Technology
Headhunters and How to Use Them
Mapping the Markets
Marketing
Organisation Culture
Successful Strategy Execution
The World of Business

Directors: an A–Z Guide
Economics: an A–Z Guide
Investment: an A–Z Guide
Negotiation: an A–Z Guide

Pocket World in Figures

# DOING BUSINESS IN CHINA
## A guide to the risks and the rewards

**Chris Torrens**

THE ECONOMIST IN ASSOCIATION WITH
PROFILE BOOKS LTD

Published by Profile Books Ltd
3A Exmouth House, Pine Street, London EC1R 0JH
*www.profilebooks.com*

Typeset in EcoType by MacGuru Ltd
*info@macguru.org.uk*

Printed in Great Britain by
Clays, Bungay, Suffolk

A CIP catalogue record for this book is available
from the British Library

ISBN 978 1 84668 281 0

The paper this book is printed on is certified by the © 1996 Forest Stewardship
Council A.C. (FSC). It is ancient-forest friendly. The printer holds FSC chain of custody
SGS-COC-2061

FSC
Mixed Sources
Product group from well-managed
forests and other controlled sources

Cert no. SGS-COC-2061
www.fsc.org
© 1996 Forest Stewardship Council

To Sam, Maya and Rocco, without whom I couldn't have written this book; and to Cag, for introducing me to China

# Contents

# List of figures

# List of maps

# List of tables

乌鲁木齐
Urumqi

新疆
XINJIANG

甘肅
GANSU

青海
QINGHAI

西藏
TIBET

拉薩
Lhasa

雲南
YUNNA

## A NOTE ON CITY CLASSIFICATION

China's statisticians categorise the country's cities according to administrative criteria: the four centrally controlled municipalities (Beijing, Shanghai, Tianjin and Chongqing); 27 provincial capitals; and 310 prefecture cities. Within the municipality, provincial capitals and prefecture cities' territory are 856 urban districts, 369 county-level cities and 1,600 counties.

This segmentation can confuse investors, who have created their own versions. The categorisation used in this book is as follows:[1]

- First tier – four municipalities, 27 provincial capitals and a few prosperous prefecture cities such as Shenzhen, Dalian and Ningbo.
- Second tier – over 300 prefecture-level cities.
- Third tier – 1,200 urban districts and county-level cities.
- Fourth tier – 1,600 counties.

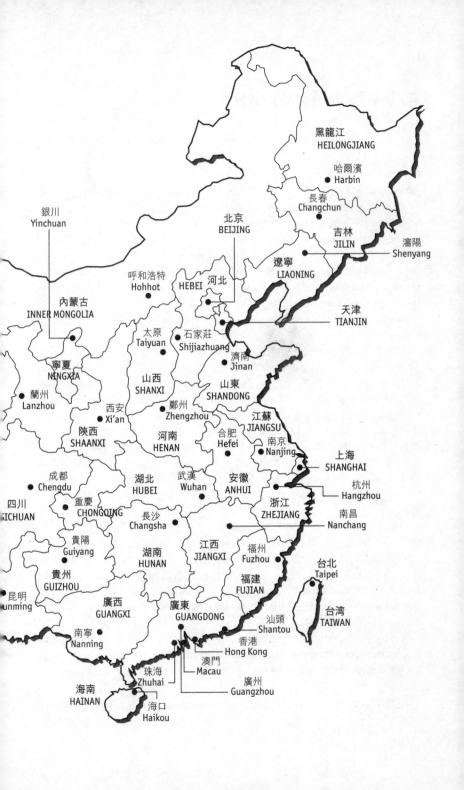

# Acknowledgements

This book relies heavily on research I have carried out over the past 12 years on behalf of the Economist Intelligence Unit. Special thanks go to Elizabeth Cheng, the Economist Intelligence Unit's *China Hand* editor, and Gaddi Tam, who generously provided information and data for many of the chapters. *China Hand* is a comprehensive guide to China's political, economic and business environment with information updated on a regular basis. It contains case studies focusing on the commercial success strategies and failures of major international blue-chip companies in China, and provides a valuable guide to China's complex laws and regulations. For more details contact: Elizabeth Cheng (elizabethcheng@economist.com).

I am grateful to all those who contributed advice, comments and quotes. They include, in no particular order: Carolyn Schofield, Jane Duckett, Stephen Green, Xing Xiaoming, Tim Clissold, Ian Maskell, John Williams, Peter Goodman, Marco Gentili, John Leary, Arthur Kroeber, Simon Cartledge, Jean-Michel Dumont, Chris Kaye, Andrew Gilholm, Emmanuel Bonhomme, Barry Colman, Sam Crispin, Paul French, Matthew Crabbe, Zhao Yiwei, Benjamin Simar, Robert Taylor, David Foster, Nick Carter, Tim Summers, Doris Ma, Zhu Sheng, Liu Xiaoyang, Jonathan Hardy, Tom Doctoroff, Paul Husband, Daniel Rosen, Charles Webb, Paul Bromberg, Greg Rumney, Michael Fosh, Chris Hunter, Jane Parry, John Bray and Dom Chester.

My classmates at the China-Europe International Business School provided a wealth of experiences and insights in many different sectors and businesses in 2006–08. I am also particularly grateful to Stephen Brough for guiding me through the entire project, and to Penny Williams for her patience and excellent editing. Any mistakes and inaccuracies in the book are my own. Similarly, the views expressed in this book are my own and not necessarily those of Control Risks Group Limited.

Lastly, I would like to thank my wife, Sam, for pushing me to write this book and supporting me throughout; and my children, Maya and Rocco, for patiently putting up with my absence on all those lost weekends.

Chris Torrens
*May 2010*

# Preface

China's emergence as a global superpower has taken place with almost indecent haste. The past three decades of market reforms have unleashed economic growth of a scale and pace almost unprecedented in history. Economic development has brought with it increasingly complex political, social and environmental challenges, yet the roller-coaster ride continues as the ruling political elite maintains a fine balance between growth and control. China has emerged from the global economic crisis even stronger than before. Not only is it a global manufacturing hub for cost-cutting multinationals; it is also emerging as significant consumer market – though the transition from investment to consumption will take many years to complete.

The aim of this book is to help all those doing business in, or with, China to avoid some of the mistakes made by their predecessors. It attempts to cover every step that companies need to consider, using case studies and examples to illustrate points and comments from executives with experience of the market.

---

**Exchange rate**

Amounts of money in renminbi have been converted to US dollars at the rate of Rmb6.8 to $1.

---

# 1 Making it work in China

Experience is the name everyone gives to their mistakes.

Oscar Wilde

China has a long history of confounding multinational companies. Many companies have relied on their strategies for developed markets to operate in the country. For most this has failed, and they have been forced to revise plans to take into account the idiosyncrasies of the Chinese market. This chapter examines the strategies that have succeeded (as well as those that have failed). It assesses the real importance of establishing and maintaining relationships (*guanxi*) in ensuring business success. And it addresses the challenge of managing corporate expectations by communicating these realities effectively to company boards and shareholders.

About 480 *Fortune* 500 companies are already in China, according to *Harvard Business Review*. More than 90% of multinational companies say that China is important to their global strategies, with 52% calling it critical. For some multinationals, such as US carmaker General Motors, French retailer Carrefour and US fast-food giant KFC, China is their largest overseas market. For others, the fact that China will eventually become the world's largest consumer market makes it an unmissable opportunity. Around 70% of the world's leading 50 retailers have entered the Chinese market. With an economy three times the size of the economies of the other BRIC[1] countries (Brazil, Russia and India) added together, China is a country that cannot be ignored.

Multinationals source goods from China in a bid to gain scale and cost efficiencies. The combination of low-cost manufacturing, modernising infrastructure, increasingly standardised tariffs and political stability – not to mention an attractive consumer market – makes China one of the best options in the world for sourcing operations. Other markets offer cheaper manufacturing costs but fall down on supply chain costs and security.

China's manufacturing costs may have risen, but the country is unlikely to lose its status as a centre for global sourcing because of its abundant supplies of cheap land and labour, and the massive long-term potential of its domestic market. In 2009 Intel, a US chipmaker, closed plants in Malaysia and the Philippines but elected to remain in China, albeit shifting its manufacturing sites from the wealthy coastal areas to inland provinces, where land and labour costs are lower. Like Japan, Hong Kong and Taiwan before it, China has used its attractions as a cheap manufacturing base to bolster economic growth. Yet China's uniqueness lies in the size and pace of its growth, both unprecedented in history. Foreign companies have played an integral part in modern China's development. Foreign-invested businesses now account for 30% of industrial output, 55% of trade and 11% of urban jobs, contributing hugely to China's overriding goal of economic development.

In the 1970s, China had gained some limited experience of dealing with the outside world by engaging private companies from Canada, France, Germany, Italy, Japan and the UK to import plants in industries such as agrochemicals, iron and steel, and power generation. But it was in the 1980s that foreign investment took off, led by Hong Kong and Taiwanese investment in export-processing capacity, which created pockets of intense growth in the southern provinces of Fujian and Guangdong, particularly in the Pearl River Delta and the nascent special economic zones. In the 1990s, US, European and East Asian (particularly Japanese, followed by South Korean) investment started to grow in the south and in the Yangtze River Delta on the east coast, spurred by the re-emergence of Shanghai as an international investment destination and the creation of Pudong New Area – the site of the Shanghai Stock Exchange, which reopened in 1990 after a 41-year break. In the 2000s, foreign investment and economic development accelerated in these two areas and also spread northwards to the capital, Beijing, and its nearest port, Tianjin, helped largely by China's long-awaited accession into the World Trade Organisation (WTO) in 2001 and its subsequent integration into the global economy.

These regions, which once relied on attracting foreign capital to build export-processing manufacturing plants through cheap land and labour, can now afford to be more selective about foreign investment. Rather than accepting any investment whatsoever, the government now seeks to attract investment that benefits its own social, economic and environmental policies, along with stringent operating standards. Export processing, which typically involves low value added, is no longer seen as a valuable component of the national economy, particularly in the wake of the global recession. The government is also increasingly sensitive towards resource-hungry, environmentally unfriendly industries such as chemicals, publishing and paper, clustering such projects in industrial parks typically some distance from major urban areas.

One of China's long-term goals is innovation. The country was once the most innovative and technologically advanced nation in the world, 1,000 years ahead of Europe in the invention of printing, windmills, mechanical clocks, gunpowder and porcelain. By the 15th century it was building 8,000-tonne ships capable of sailing around the world. Yet now China is known as the workshop of the world, assembling and replicating foreign products. Its goal is to move up the innovation ladder and away from the old assembly lines that built southern China's wealth. Taking a leaf out of the book of developed nations (research and development accounts for 2.7% of US GDP), it set a target of 2.5% for R&D spending as a proportion of national GDP by 2012. By 2007, such spending accounted for 1.4% of GDP. Over 300 multinational companies have opened R&D centres in China, particularly in sectors such as pharmaceuticals and information technology. Roche, Pfizer, Novartis, Microsoft, Sony and Samsung have all set up R&D centres on the mainland, even if their focus is more 'D' than 'R' – with some multinationals choosing to develop existing technologies rather than research sensitive new ones, partly because of concerns about intellectual property protection.

By emphasising R&D and priority sectors such as technology, renewable energy and services, the government hopes to move away from low-value-added to high-value-added sectors. This is already a painful reality for some provincial governments. In Guangdong, for example, rising land and labour costs have left the authorities with too few workers, forcing companies to turn to new higher-value-added products to survive. Dongguan, a conglomeration of at least seven towns, has become the province's third-largest city by gobbling up the paddy fields that once separated the provincial capital Guangzhou from the special economic zone of Shenzhen on the southern border with Hong Kong. In its urban sprawl, as many as 40% of the factories churning out goods for export had shut down by the end of 2008 in response to rising prices, new regulations governing product safety and the onset of the global financial crisis, which reduced international demand.

China's transformation from a labour-intensive to a capital-intensive economy will see a shift to the production of higher value-added goods, supported by an expanding urban middle class with real consumer power. Yet this (still swift) evolution will take decades, rather than years, to complete. Surveys carried out by the European Union Chamber of Commerce in China and the US-China Business Council[2] in 2009 illustrated growing investor concern that was losing its competitive edge because of rising labour and regulatory costs. Yet while China's relatively affluent coastal areas may be less competitive, inland regions will continue to offer cheap land and labour for multinational and local companies with labour-intensive, export-driven manufacturing needs. These advantages will help maintain high levels of foreign direct investment (FDI) inflows and manufacturing for export, assisted by continuing state investment in infrastructure.

China has swiftly left behind the diplomatic tussles that accompanied its first few years as a WTO member. Where once it was upbraided for dragging its heels to reach the required level of compliance, now foreign governments are focusing on getting the best price for their natural resources from Chinese state companies desperate to secure global energy and resource supplies to feed their burgeoning economy. Such acquisitions can be politically sensitive, with many politicians wary of what they see as the government's strategic (rather than purely commercial) intentions.

## Less (political) risk, more (economic) reward

The impact of the global recession on political and economic stability has prompted a reappraisal of China's overall stability in comparison to other countries. According to a special report published in 2009 by the Economist Intelligence Unit assessing the extent of political distress arising from the global crisis, China suffered from a lower level of political instability than many of the 165 countries covered – including the United States, France and Spain.[3] The Economist Intelligence Unit's Political Instability Index rates countries on an overall index on a scale of 0 (no vulnerability) to 10 (highest vulnerability) based upon two principal components: underlying vulnerability and economic distress. Those Asian countries in the high-risk category are: Bangladesh; Indonesia; North Korea; Pakistan; the Philippines; and Thailand.

## Strategies

A number of tricky choices face China investors. Do they:

- take that first-mover advantage and be the first to enter virgin territory, or wait for others to make mistakes before entering;
- dip a foot in the water with a soft launch in one local market, or make a big front-page splash across several provinces;
- opt for a joint-venture partner to help navigate awkward areas such as distribution and government relations, or go it alone with the freedom of a wholly owned operation;
- hit the ground running through acquisition or existing operations or build their operation from a greenfield site?

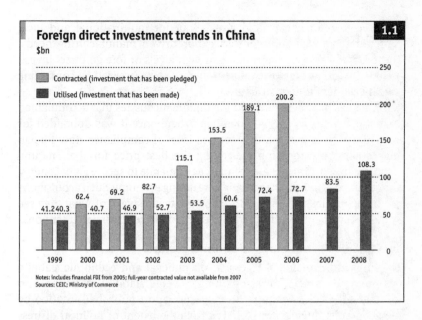

**Foreign direct investment trends in China** 1.1
$bn

- Contracted (investment that has been pledged)
- Utilised (investment that has been made)

Notes: includes financial FDI from 2005; full-year contracted value not available from 2007
Sources: CEIC; Ministry of Commerce

Multinational companies have taken every conceivable route to the Chinese market, with staggeringly different results. There is of course no single strategy to guarantee success, but there are some clear steps that investors should take before (and while) investing in China. These are set out in detail in Chapters 3–9. This chapter contains examples of some successful, and some not so successful, strategies adopted by foreign investors over the past two decades.

Thousands of companies have worked out ways of doing business in China. Each has doubtless encountered obstacles, often seemingly insurmountable, but negotiated these and learned from the experience to create stronger and ultimately more successful operations. As one long-term British resident of Shanghai says:

> With sufficient ambition anything can be achieved in China: "anything", of course, includes disaster and entrants must take time to identify the risks and prepare strategies to quickly respond to the pitfalls.

The key to success is to learn from difficult experiences, mistakes and failures.

This was certainly the case with early entrants to the market. After

Table 1.1 **Economist Intelligence Unit Political Stability Index: selected countries, 2009–10**

| Rank | Country | Underlying vulnerability | Economic distress | Index score | 2007 score |
|------|---------|--------------------------|-------------------|-------------|------------|
| 1 | Zimbabwe | 7.5 | 10.0 | 8.8 | 8.8 |
| 2 | Chad | 7.1 | 10.0 | 8.5 | 7.5 |
| 3 | Congo (Dem Rep) | 8.3 | 8.0 | 8.2 | 7.2 |
| 4 | Cambodia | 7.9 | 8.0 | 8.0 | 6.0 |
| 4 | Sudan | 7.9 | 8.0 | 8.0 | 7.0 |
| 6 | Iraq | 8.8 | 7.0 | 7.9 | 7.9 |
| 7 | Côte d'Ivoire | 7.5 | 8.0 | 7.8 | 7.8 |
| 7 | Haïti | 7.5 | 8.0 | 7.8 | 6.8 |
| 7 | Pakistan | 7.5 | 8.0 | 7.8 | 5.8 |
| 7 | Zambia | 7.5 | 8.0 | 7.8 | 6.8 |
| 7 | Afghanistan | 7.5 | 8.0 | 7.8 | 6.8 |
| 7 | Central African Republic | 7.5 | 8.0 | 7.8 | 5.8 |
| 13 | North Korea | 5.4 | 10.0 | 7.7 | 3.7 |
| 14 | Bolivia | 8.3 | 7.0 | 7.7 | 5.7 |
| 33 | Myanmar | 6.3 | 8.0 | 7.1 | 4.1 |
| 52 | Indonesia | 6.7 | 7.0 | 6.8 | 3.8 |
| 54 | Philippines | 4.6 | 9.0 | 6.8 | 4.8 |
| 66 | Russia | 5.0 | 8.0 | 6.5 | 3.4 |
| 83 | Mongolia | 4.2 | 8.0 | 6.1 | 4.0 |
| 105 | Brazil | 5.8 | 5.0 | 5.4 | 4.4 |
| 110 | France | 2.5 | 8.0 | 5.3 | 1.3 |
| 110 | United States | 2.5 | 8.0 | 5.3 | 3.2 |
| 117 | South Korea | 4.2 | 6.0 | 5.1 | 2.0 |
| 121 | Italy | 2.1 | 8.0 | 5.0 | 4.9 |
| 124 | China | 4.6 | 5.0 | 4.8 | 3.8 |
| 130 | Singapore | 3.3 | 6.0 | 4.7 | 1.7 |
| 132 | United Kingdom | 1.3 | 8.0 | 4.6 | 0.6 |
| 135 | India | 5.0 | 4.0 | 4.5 | 4.5 |

Source: http://viewswire.eiu.com/site_info.asp?info_name=social_unrest_table&page=noads

eyeing the mainland market since the 1970s, General Motors set up its first manufacturing operation (making transmissions) in China in 1984 via its automotive subsidiary, General Motors Automobile Corporation (GMAC). GMAC's goal was to build entire vehicles, and in 1992 it unveiled a joint venture with state-owned Jinbei Automobile Co in Shenyang (north-eastern Liaoning province) to build compact pick-up trucks. This was described at the time by the *New American* magazine as one of the largest US investments in China following the Tian'anmen Square crackdown of 1989.[4] GMAC designed a four-seater utility model for farm or small-business use with an open-crate back, but kitted out the cabin with the finest leather upholstering that had proved so popular with customers back home. Less than a dozen were sold. But GM persevered, setting up other truck (and later car) production plants, eventually cracking the market with the launch of the Buick sedan. China is now GM's largest market after the United States. GM is the leading manufacturer in the Chinese market, with more than 1m vehicles sold by its various joint ventures in 2007, followed by Volkswagen with just over 900,000 vehicles. Crucially, foreign investors such as GM and Volkswagen have had to adapt to the evolving market. In 1998, 83% of cars sold in China were bought by the state; by 2008, 83% of car sales were to private buyers – far more demanding consumers.[5]

Size clearly matters. Multinational investors in China need long-term plans (and big budgets) to succeed. A British businessman based in Shanghai for ten years believes it helps if you are already a global operator:

> *Essentially you have to be huge already to succeed here – being*
> *small doesn't work. As a specialist you may be successful –*
> *though you will be copied. You really have to be big enough (and*
> *have deep enough pockets) to try, fail, learn and try again.*

Like many smaller companies with a quality product, Hornby, a venerable British manufacturer of classic toy train sets, had no choice but to move. Enjoying a renaissance thanks to the Hogwarts Express featuring in the Harry Potter films, Hornby took the decision to move its production to China, keeping just its designers and managers in the UK's head office in Margate. In speaking about the benefits of the move, Hornby's CEO says:[6]

> *The strain on the bottom line began to ease immediately. We*
> *were able to use the savings to increase the quality and details of*
> *the models so that sales began to pick up.*

The reality is that the company would have been forced to close if it had not taken this option.

## Pioneer investors: the early years

Following the establishment of the People's Republic of China in 1949, western companies wasted little time in seeking to forge links with the new administration. In 1953–54, a collection of British companies and business representatives that became known as the 48 Group (and which is still active today) made two visits to Beijing in a bid to lift an international trade embargo imposed on the communist regime following the overthrow of Chiang Kai-shek's Nationalist government. Yet it was almost 20 more years before western governments were prepared to re-engage with China. In the wake of US President Richard Nixon's historic visit to Beijing in 1972 and the subsequent resumption of diplomatic relations, a handful of US companies won contracts in China. M.W. Kellogg sold eight ammonia plants to China for the production of fertiliser, and aircraft builder Boeing sold ten 707 airliners and opened a representative office (albeit short-lived) in Beijing.

The following year the first British Trade and Industry Exhibition took place in Beijing, opened by Michael Heseltine, the trade and industry minister, and featuring dozens of British companies, such as Rolls-Royce, which displayed its Concorde aircraft engine. The British prime minister, Edward Heath, visited Mao Zedong in Beijing twice in 1974 and 1975, and in the latter year Rolls-Royce sold China a licence to manufacture the Spey engine, which had been used in British phantom fighters. Marconi, GEC's defence subsidiary, was also involved. Three years later, Henry Ford II met the then vice-premier, Deng Xiaoping; Mercedes-Benz, Fiat and British Leyland also sent delegations to the country.

In 1980, French President Giscard d'Estaing visited China, in part to promote a French nuclear company, Framatome, for the Daya Bay nuclear contract. (Framatome would eventually win the deal.) Three years later, French President François Mitterrand visited China with a similar message of support. In 1984, German Chancellor Helmut Kohl visited China with representatives of Siemens. In the same year Beijing also hosted US President Ronald Reagan and a contingent of US corporate giants such as American Express, American Motors Corporation, Bechtel, Boeing, Chase Manhattan, Exxon, Fluor Corporation, General Electric, Hewlett-Packard, Honeywell, IBM, Kodak and Westinghouse.

Foreign investors were attracted by China's untapped market, despite the riskiness of these early ventures. When in 1980 the Chinese government found that it could not afford a multibillion-dollar steel construction project for Baoshan Steel, it cancelled it, leaving Japan's Nippon Steel and Mitsubishi, and Germany's

Mannesman-Demag and Scholesman-Siemag with unpaid bills. Other major plans remained on the drawing board, including a proposed aluminium plant involving Bechtel and a plan by Fluor for what would have been the world's largest copper mine. Meanwhile, BP drilled 14 wells in the South China Sea in the early 1980s but all were dry.

Coca-Cola was one of the first global consumer brands to enter the modern Chinese market in the early 1980s. When it opened its bottling plants in Beijing the company was forced to sell most of its product to tourists and other foreigners – who were required to use foreign exchange certificates (*waihuiquan*) rather than the non-convertible local currency, the renminbi[7] – in order to gain the foreign exchange needed to import concentrates from abroad.

In 1984, German carmaker Volkswagen made its debut with the Santana sedan, manufactured by a new joint venture with Shanghai Automotive Industry Corporation. (Fifteen years later, 48 out of every 100 cars sold in China would be Santanas; and even in 2010, customers in inland provinces were still buying Santanas because they prefer an affordable passenger car with four doors, rather than just two. The following year, GM became one of the first US corporations to set up manufacturing operations in China via a ten-year deal between its Detroit Diesel Allison subsidiary and state-run Qijiang Gear Works in Chongqing (then in Sichuan province) to build transmissions. (GM would start manufacturing trucks in 1992 via a joint venture with Shenyang-based Jinbei Automobile.) By the first half of the 1980s automobile manufacturers were importing into China: France's Citroën and Peugeot; Italy's Fiat; and Japan's Nissan and Toyota (annual exports from Japan increased sevenfold to 85,000 in 1984 alone).

Japanese imports in consumer electronics were also impressive. Imports of television sets in 1984 increased sevenfold to 2.3m, twice as many as Japan sold to the United States in the same year. The following year, a 100-member delegation from the Japanese Chamber of Commerce toured China.

By the mid-1980s, more consumer brands were finding their way into the market: international camera film brands Kodak and Agfa were widely available across the country by 1984, competing against the local favourite, Lucky (*lekai*). When, after four years of preparation, US company Nabisco launched a new venture with local food producer Yili in 1985 to sell cracker biscuits in China, it brought over 2 tonnes of Nabisco products for its business partners to taste. The result of this somewhat limited market research exercise was the launch of Ritz crackers and Premium Saltines on the local market. The same year, Otis Elevator signed one of the country's first joint ventures in the port city of Tianjin, near Beijing. By this time Rothmans was manufacturing cigarettes using Molins technology and joint ventures (albeit ones in which foreigners were restricted to minority stakes) were increasingly common.

## The retailers

Around 35 of the world's top 50 retailers are in China. Yet even the largest players have only a tiny percentage of this hugely fragmented market. The vast majority of retail outlets are the tiny, independent (usually family-run) stores or kiosks (*xiaomaibu*) to be found on every street corner and in every village across the country.[8] In the cities, the fight for market share dominates various retail categories – supermarkets, department stores, home improvements, home appliances – which provide some enlightening examples of successes and failures.

The world's top three retailers, Wal-Mart, Carrefour and Tesco, adopted widely differing entry and growth strategies. Wal-Mart (number one) and Carrefour (number two) entered the Chinese market in the mid-1990s, with US retailer Wal-Mart focusing on Shenzhen on the southern border with Hong Kong and French retailer Carrefour opening further north in Beijing and Shanghai. As retail restrictions were slowly lifted in the wake of China's WTO accession at the end of 2001, Carrefour expanded aggressively – and beyond the terms of the regulatory rollout – by setting up joint ventures in provinces where local governments were prepared to ignore central rules in order to attract prestigious investors. The retailer was penalised for its actions, but the benefits of bending the rules far outweighed the punishment. In late 2005 it bought out its Kunming-based joint-venture partner, creating Carrefour's first wholly owned foreign enterprise (WOFE) in China, and by the third quarter of 2009 was operating 145 mainland stores.

By contrast, Wal-Mart played a cautious game, restricting its operations to Guangdong until it made a cautious expansion out of the province in the early 2000s as retail restrictions were slowly lifted. In 2007 Wal-Mart acquired a local chain, Trust Mart, for $1 billion, boosting its expansion programme and enabling it to get within sight of Carrefour. By 2009, it had overtaken Carrefour, with a network of 160 stores across the country – including at least 30 new outlets in 2008 alone.

Meanwhile, Tesco, the UK's largest retailer, took a different route. Eschewing the early-bird option, the world number three bided its time before making a late entry into the (now unrestricted) market through the acquisition of a 50% stake (and 47 stores) in the Hymall chain, a subsidiary of Taiwan's Ting Hsin International Group,[9] increasing its stake to 90% in 2006. Tesco bought into Hymall's understanding of the mainland retail environment – specifically its supply and distribution networks – in a bid to catch up with the first movers. By late 2009, Tesco had 65 mainland hypermarkets (and plans for 18 more by early 2010), with nearly 20 in Shanghai alone, controlling just under 3% of the national retail market. Mergers and acquisitions also present great opportunities to grow networks in one fell swoop. French supermarket retailer Auchan, the 14th largest retailer in the world, operates more than 130 "big-box" hypermarkets (typically large-scale discount stores for bulk buying) in China, 110 of them under the brand name RT Mart in a joint venture with a Taiwanese partner. Auchan is aiming to become the largest food retailer in China.

China is not only attracting supermarkets. In the world of home improvements, Home Depot of the United States, IKEA of Sweden and B&Q of the UK are active in the mainland market. IKEA took the early-mover route, quietly opening its first mainland store in Shanghai in 1998. The soft launch was a deliberate ploy to address any teething troubles before the local and international media arrived in force for the grand opening. It also gave IKEA a chance to gauge public reaction to its product range, store location and shopping environment, enabling it to fine-tune its operations quickly and without fuss. Initially, most sales were small-ticket merchandise such as kitchenware, but with the emergence of an urban middle class together with government policies to encourage home-buying IKEA's business gained momentum. Yet expansion has been slow, with six stores as of mid-2009 and two more planned.

Another global player, B&Q (part of the UK's Kingfisher Group), entered China in 1999 on the back of a successful expansion into Taiwan. It followed the suburban "big-box" model but found that few customers had the inclination (or the private transport) to shop for branded home-improvements products, opting instead to buy cheap, generic products from small, local hardware vendors (or let their contractors do it). B&Q responded by shifting into the furnishings category (IKEA's traditional territory), setting up "decoration centres" where homebuyers could select their preferred decor for their new apartments, which are typically sold with no decoration at all. The retailer's aggressive expansion and big-box format proved optimistic, prompting it to close one-third of its 60 or so stores in 2009 and to restructure the remaining outlets.

Did B&Q and IKEA enter the market too early? The world's largest home improvements retailer, Home Depot, made its long-delayed entry into China in 2006 through the acquisition of a local home decoration retailer, Homeway, and its 12-store network. Yet three years later Home Depot was still trying to work out the best way forward amid a slump in local business. The tough reality for these operators is that Chinese consumers are not yet ready for foreign home-improvement brands, failing to attach the same value to brands in this sector as they do to, say, pharmaceuticals or cars. As a result, the market remains highly fragmented, with local businesses operating low-margin stores rented from developers. In 2007, A.T. Kearney, a consulting company, estimated that the top four branded outlets – B&Q, IKEA, Oriental Home and Home Mart – controlled just 2.5% of the market.

Consumer electronics is perhaps the toughest market to enter because of the plethora of local players. In this dog-eat-dog world the largest players, Gome and Suning, have survived only by reducing margins and engaging in a grow-or-die race to achieve economies of scale. (Such is the power of the home appliance giants that in 2007 US computer-maker Dell chose to supplement its online model with sales of its products through Gome, capitalising on its 200-city reach.) It was into this nest of vipers that the world's largest home appliance dealer, Best Buy of the United States, jumped in 2006 through the acquisition of a 75% stake in Five-Star Appliance (at the time the fifth largest local home appliance company) and its 170-store network for $184m; it acquired the remaining 25% for $185m in 2009.

However, Best Buy had been circling the market and assessing potential merger and acquisition targets before it made its move. It subsequently expanded cautiously, opening a handful of self-branded stores in the Shanghai area before stepping up its expansion plans in 2009. According to Paul French, co-founder and director of Access Asia, a business intelligence and market research firm, Best Buy remains vulnerable in the market because the market shares of the two local giants, Gome and Suning, will be hard to erode. However, French believes Best Buy can take advantage of the relative inflexibility of its rivals (especially Gome) by adapting swiftly to market changes and making on-the-ground innovations. The company's "Geek Squad" of technical support service staff did not transfer to the Chinese market successfully and needs to be repackaged for Chinese shoppers.

China has attracted department stores since the early 1990s when local consumers started to shop for pleasure rather than necessity. The absence of comfortable shopping environments attracted regional players such as Parkson, a subsidiary of the Lion Group and operator of Malaysia's largest retail chain. Parkson's first mainland store, which opened in Beijing in 1994, was filled with luxury goods priced way beyond the means of the consumers, who came to gawp at the price tags before leaving. Parkson withdrew from the market in 1996, but was soon back with a more sensibly priced mix of household items that appealed to

Shanghai's rapidly expanding middle-income segment. More thoughtful market selection and a reworked inventory helped Parkson survive and prosper after its early mistakes. By 2008, the company was operating 41 stores in 26 mainland cities.

Parkson was not alone in misjudging the market in the 1990s. Many retailers were unable to recover from their mistakes. Some foreign players were simply too early for the market, overestimating local consumer demand. In 1992, Yaohan of Japan became the first foreign company to receive a retail import licence. Yaohan's chairman, Kazuo Wada, invested a hefty $350m in the market, boasting that he would open 1,000 super-markets in the Yangtze River Delta by 2005. But by 1997, just 33 outlets had opened. In the same year Yaohan collapsed, and in 1999 Wada received a three-year jail term for accounting irregularities. The previous year another Japanese operator, Seiyu, had been forced to pull out of a joint venture to roll out department stores. Also in 1998, Dutch retailer Royal Ahold, which had been planning to build a national network from its Shanghai base of 16 stores, was forced to withdraw from the market. Nor were all the lessons learnt. More than a decade later, new players were still entering the market poorly prepared and with unrealistic expectations of China. In 2007–08 Isetan Mitsukoshi Holdings was forced to close two stores but continued to hope against hope that major Chinese cities, already saturated with huge, high-end department stores, could somehow absorb more.

**Not quite right**

*Danone: know your partner*

French food and drink manufacturer Danone entered China in 1996 with an investment in Wahaha, a private drinks company based in Hangzhou, Zhejiang. In 2006, a dispute started between the two companies based on Wahaha's independent opening of its own joint ventures, which Danone claimed contravened the terms of their initial agreement. At one point Wahaha's 40 or so parallel operations (in which Danone had no stake even though the entities were under the Wahaha brand) were costing the French partner an estimated $25m a month in lost revenues. Three years later, the two sides finally reached a settlement, with Danone relinquishing its 51% stake in the China joint venture. (In 2006 China accounted for 11% of Danone's $22 billion global sales, making it the group's third largest market after France and Spain.) This agonising experience has influenced Danone's strategy in other emerging markets: the company announced in 2009 that it would pursue growth in India on its own, pulling out of a problematic 13-year joint venture with Wadia Group, a local entity.

The bitterness of this fight was a reminder to foreign companies of some of the pitfalls of China joint ventures. Yet with hindsight, Danone made some elementary mistakes in its venture with Wahaha and its chairman, Zong Qinghou. Having invested heavily in Zong's business, the French side took little or no interest in day-to-day operations; less than a handful of Danone employees had regular access to the joint venture. Danone's hands-off attitude was misinterpreted by its partner as arrogance. The company had no sense of Zong's growing dissatisfaction with what he perceived to be effectively a "sleeping" foreign partner, who benefited unfairly from his enormous efforts in building Wahaha into a national brand (conveniently overlooking the hundreds of millions of dollars invested by Danone, without which he could not have grown his business and moved into new categories). Danone should have appreciated more the risk associated with Zong's background. As a highly motivated businessman who had lost his education to the Cultural Revolution, he had learnt to trust nobody but himself; his combative personality was amply illustrated through his reputation as a strongly nationalist entrepreneur prone to jingoistic rabble-rousing; and his political trajectory into the National People's Congress, China's parliament, earned him powerful allies (and enemies) whose help he sought to enlist in his fight against Danone.

### Bertelsmann: publishing is tough

German publisher Bertelsmann shocked many in 2008 with its sudden pull-out from China, but many had seen that the book club model was not working and that too much competition in a market with narrow margins was not going to be sustainable. First it had to close its bookstore chain (36 stores in 18 cities) after a bricks-and-mortar book retailing disaster, with the German headquarters eventually deciding to pull the plug. The book club did not last much longer. Despite years of effort and funding, China remained the smallest market out of 56 for Bertelsmann's Direct Group. Most agree that its purchase of the Beijing 21st Century Jinxiu Bookstore franchise was the fatal flaw, and this only added to the strain on margins. Bertelsmann insists it is still committed to the China market, but this has little to do with bookselling and more to do with other media products.

### Marks & Spencer: if at first you don't succeed

UK department store Marks & Spencer spent well over a decade assessing the Chinese market before finally opening shortly before Christmas 2008. The company has enjoyed considerable success in the Hong Kong market with basic, middle-of-the-road apparel and accessories, but its Shanghai opening was marred by some bad luck (never good in the eyes of superstitious Chinese consumers) in the form of a fatal accident on the escalator of its flagship Shanghai store. The company, which has suffered a decline at home, plans to expand in China, with more stores in Shanghai and new outlets in Beijing and Shenzhen.

## Clash of the global titans

Like other emerging markets, China is a battleground for global brands, particularly the famous duels fought in frontier markets over the decades: Coca-Cola versus Pepsi; McDonald's versus KFC; Unilever versus Procter & Gamble; Microsoft versus Apple.

### Coke the king, Pepsi the pretender

The contest between Coca-Cola and Pepsi has lasted 20 years in China, though Coke has been the undisputed king since it first arrived at the start of the 1980s. Coca-Cola's growth in popularity was helped by its brand colour, red (a traditional Chinese favourite symbolising celebration), and by its Chinese brand name, *kekou kele* (literally "drink and be happy"), an inspired transliteration that the company had registered as a trademark when it first entered the Chinese market back in 1928. By 2009, Coca-Cola had at least 37 bottling plants in China, which was its third largest market globally.

By contrast, Pepsi entered the market some time after Coca-Cola and with a less memorable Chinese brand name. Yet while it has traditionally lacked the instant appeal of its global rival, Pepsi's tireless marketing campaigns have helped it gradually gain ground to the point where it trails Coca-Cola only marginally in its share of China's cola market.[10] Much of Pepsi's success has come from connecting more successfully with youth consumers through "viral" marketing, while also tapping into nationalist emotions with its acclaimed "Go China" campaign during the 2008 Olympic Games.

Pepsi also benefited indirectly from the Chinese government's decision in 2009 to reject Coca-Cola's $2.4 billion bid for a controlling stake in China Huiyuan Juice, which controls 40% of the local pure fruit-juice market. This was a shock for foreign investors. Many saw rejection of the deal by the Ministry of Commerce (Mofcom) on the grounds that it would have curbed competition as a demonstration of China's keenness to protect home-grown brands; others believed that the public outcry – seen most clearly in internet chatrooms and on bulletin boards – at encroaching foreign ownership of local brands prompted Mofcom to make the move.

Table 1.2 **Some fast-food brand chains, August 2009**

| Brand | Year established in China | No. of outlets | Expansion plans |
|---|---|---|---|
| KFC | 1987 | 2,600 | 370 new outlets in 2009 |
| McDonald's | 1990 | 850 | 500 new outlets by 2011 |
| Pizza Hut | 1990 | 430 | 10–15 outlets per year plus additional home-delivery stations |
| Little Sheep | 1999 | 376 | 60 new outlets in 2009 |
| Kung Fu | 2002 | 270 | Planned stockmarket listing |
| Yoshinoya | 1992 | 211 | 1,000 outlets by 2013 |
| Dairy Queen | 1992 | 170 | 100 new outlets in 2009 |
| Subway | 1995 | 128 | Actively seeking franchisees |
| Papa John's Pizza | 2003 | 118 | 250 outlets by 2011 |
| 85 Degrees | 2007 | 42 | 91 new outlets by 2010 |
| East Dawning | 2005 | 18 | None announced |
| Burger King | 2005 | 12 | 300 new outlets by 2011 |
| Dunkin' Donuts | 2008 | 6 | 100 outlets by 2011 |

Source: Access Asia from company information

Whatever the reasons behind the decision, Coca-Cola's loss has been Pepsi's gain. Pepsi, which planned to invest $1 billion in China in 2009–12, spent $5m sponsoring the US exhibition area at the 2010 Shanghai World Expo, despite the fact that its rival Coca-Cola was global sponsor for the event and sole distributor of soft drinks at outlets on the Expo site. In 2009, Coca-Cola responded with a $2 billion, three-year investment plan for China, opening two new bottling plants that year.

### Chicken is a winner
In another huge contest, KFC and McDonald's have been head-to-head since the mid-1980s. KFC arrived first, opening its first, cavernous outlet in Beijing in 1987. McDonald's followed in 1992 but would always be at a disadvantage in a market where chicken is universally popular but beef is rarely eaten. By mid-2009, KFC had some 2,600 outlets in 550 cities – contributing a whopping 20% to global company revenues – and had plans to open a store a day in 2010. KFC is still ruler of the roost but increasingly

faces competition from smaller, fast-improving local operators: Kung Fu (Zheng Gongfu), with its Bruce Lee logo; East Dawning, a new western-style fast-food chain serving up staple Chinese dishes (owned by Yum! Brands, the US owner of KFC, Pizza Hut and Taco Bell); and Little Sheep, a popular chain of Hotpot restaurants (in which Yum! owns a 20% stake).

### *Guanxi*: overhyped but still useful

The concept of "face" or "self-respect" (*mianzi*) dates back to the *Book of Songs* (*Shijing*), the earliest collection of Chinese poetry believed to have been written around 1,000BC.[11] By contrast, the related concept of *guanxi* did not even appear in dictionaries in the 1930s, though by this time it was being used in daily speech. Literally, the character which comprises "*guan*" can mean "to close" or "junction" or "check-point" (as in Shanhaiguan, the place in Hebei province where the eastern end of the Great Wall meets the Bohai Sea); "*xi*" means "to tie" or "connect", or, in its noun form, "system". Standard interpretations of *guanxi* include: "connections" or "relations", though these English translations fail to describe the full meaning of the word.

    *Guanxi* describes the personal networks that underpin all business relationships. *Guanxi* encapsulates other social behaviours including "face", the emotion of personal interaction and sentiment (*ganqing*) and the moral duty inherent in maintaining a relationship (*renqing*). The business relationship implicit in *guanxi* requires mutual co-operation by each party; this co-operation is personal and cannot be transferred to other people. John Williams, country manager at International SOS, a global medical assistance company, equates *guanxi* with networks and connections in other business cultures but believes that it can reap much more rewarding results than in other business cultures. Certainly, these relationships are not unique to China: similar concepts exist in the form of *Blat* in Russian culture,[12] *wasta* in Middle Eastern culture[13] and even the old-boy networks of western societies. Yet although informal networks exist in all societies, it can be argued that they are more prevalent in China than elsewhere. According to Lucian Pye, an author specialising in China:[14]

> *In China, a wide divide has always existed between formal government, emanating from the imperial or national capital, and the private governance that rules the daily lives of people.*

Under the terms of *guanxi*, people engage with each other as individuals rather than what Wang Hongying, author of *Weak States, Strong Networks*, calls "role occupants". It takes *ganqing* to initiate and maintain *guanxi*, which then constitute a reciprocal relationship where the repayment of favours is required, no matter how convoluted the return route to the beneficiary may be. Williams says:

> *So much dealing goes on behind the scenes in China and people will bend over backwards where a particular guanxi is concerned to help even those people they do not know ... but do it for the sake of their own guanxi.*

Companies operating in China have actively cultivated *guanxi* for commercial gain. As one Hong Kong businessman, who first set up manufacturing operations in Guangdong in the 1980s, says:

> *China is not like Hong Kong. You can't rely on the law – you have to make your way using networks of contacts.*

Another businessman maintains:

> *We know it takes at least 1–2 years to establish good guanxi, so we rotate our senior management only every 4–5 years.*

As in other cultures, *guanxi* has suffered from an association (often perceived, often real) with corruption. It is true that the line between maintaining *guanxi* and engaging in bribery can occasionally blur. Gifts such as dinner at an expensive restaurant, a bottle of whisky or a bulky *hongbao* (a red envelope given at Chinese New Year) can be interpreted by some (including the recipient) as bribery and, where applicable, a violation of international regulatory principles.

Much of the mystique of *guanxi* is misplaced. Yet it is true that business transactions in China are based to a greater extent on personal relationships, mutual understanding and implicit agreements than on formal legal contracts. In his book *Chinese Commercial Negotiating Style*, Pye says:[15]

> *The Chinese seem to have less feeling for the drama of agreement and little expectation that any formalised contract will end the process of negotiations ... for the Chinese, the very achievement of a formalised agreement, like the initial agreement on principles, means that the two parties understand each other well enough that each can expect further favours from the other.*

It is important to remember that this state of affairs stems less from a Chinese love of *guanxi* than a realisation that in China's evolving legal and administrative environments the law could not be counted on when carrying out business deals

– hence the traditional establishment of connections with family and friends. As these areas become stronger, more predictable and transparent, it is logical to assume that the need for *guanxi* will ultimately diminish, though there will always a perceived benefit to developing high-level political relationships in the hope that this will help to oil the wheels of business at some point.[16] But it is worth bearing in mind that even carefully maintained *guanxi* can be lost. As Mark Schaub, a Shanghai-based partner at local law firm King and Wood, says: "*Guanxi* get old; *guanxi* get divorced; *guanxi* die."

Three golden rules:

- Every action has a reaction. For every favour you call in through *guanxi*, you will at some point be required to return a favour, which may not be entirely to your liking.
- Never burn your bridges or your own *guanxi*. You never know when you will need that extra bit of *guanxi* to drive something through to closure.
- Find ways to build connections and networks around the country both vertically and horizontally to get maximum effect.

## Managing corporate expectations

Prospects in China often look far more attractive to foreign executives looking into China from the West or making short visits to the country than they do to the business people living in China. Even in the 1830s, British employees of the East India Company based in the southern city of Canton (modern-day Guangzhou) were in constant dispute with their British head office over the viability of much of their traded goods. The lure of the Chinese consumer stretches back hundreds of years. An English merchant in the mid-19th century said:[17]

> If we could persuade every person in China to lengthen his shirttail by a foot, we could keep the mills of Lancashire working around the clock.

In the 1930s the US Farmers' Association dreamt of "selling an apple to every Chinese". Today, more than two-thirds of foreign firms operating in China are believed to be profitable, though tax records indicate that only one-third make a profit. This suggests that some companies may be concealing their profits.

China-based managers still face numerous challenges to profitability. John Williams of International SOS has been doing business in China for

20 years. He says:

> It is essential to the success of operations in China that corporate
> expectations are managed. Very often head office can be blinded
> by the sheer scale of opportunity without appreciating the
> complexity of doing business in China. People back home often
> also forget the scale of China's geography and the distances
> involved in doing business in China. While it is true that things
> can be made to happen surprisingly quickly in China, the right
> factors need to be present: the will to get things done; a political
> agenda that is aligned with your strategy; and local partners
> who are working in the same direction as you. Head office also
> needs to remember that obstacles can appear unexpectedly to
> derail initiatives, at least temporarily.

Specific industries can be particularly tough. Chris Kaye of BCG, a
global management consulting firm, underlines the critical importance of
managing corporate expectations in the insurance industry:

> No foreign JVs are consistently making money yet, so setting
> expectations of a long j-curve is an important part of ensuring
> commitment to the market – and this goes as much for the
> foreign corporate HQ as it does for the local JV partner HQ.
> One technique is consistently to report performance on a broad
> range of KPIs [key performance indicators] related to building a
> quality business. This is especially powerful if done relative to
> other foreign players: e.g. time to sell 100k policies, productivity
> per branch, senior management retention. While profit delivery
> is one dimension, it is equally important to manage scale
> expectations as well. Although demand is large and fast growing
> in China, accessible demand tends to be much lower – either
> because of licensing restrictions, and distribution constraints,
> or because material demand is still a few years out. Creating
> long-term commitment with HQ rests on being realistic and
> clear about the time frame from the start, and then consistently
> delivering. Falling short of overambitious targets is a sure-fire
> way to undermine long-term commitment.

Elizabeth Cheng, editor of the Economist Intelligence Unit's *China Hand*,
an annual publication for China-based business executives, believes that

China continues to have the ability to "excite" and to "depress":

> The tendency is to swing to extremes, so every manager in China should make sure that head office is tuned to ground developments. To do this, good communication is required and this can be achieved through regular reporting, reviewing or teleconferencing with head office point persons and field visits.

The global downturn has raised corporate expectations as other markets falter and China continues to grow. A British veteran of the Chinese advertising industry based in Shanghai complained in 2010 that despite a growing business, he was under greater pressure to guarantee revenues than at any time during his 15 years in Greater China; with losses being incurred in other markets, his head office was keen to generate the profit margins it needs to keep the share price buoyant.

### Challenges for foreign investors

- **Domestic competition.** The emergence of significant domestic competition over the past decade reflects the speed at which local companies have climbed the learning curve – some of them aided by state subsidies. Benefiting from technology transfers, foreign capital and imported management techniques, local companies present fierce competition to foreign companies in often crowded categories. Indigenous brands, long dominant in home appliances, have also moved into foreign-held territory such as personal computers (leaving Dell of the United States as the only foreign player in the top ten brands) and mobile phones (where Motorola of the United States and Nokia of Finland have been usurped by cheaper but still innovative local brands with hefty marketing budgets). Meanwhile, some sectors – publishing, telecoms, media, insurance – remain restricted to foreign investment, giving local companies a huge advantage.
- **Loss of tax concessions.** The introduction of the Enterprise Income Tax (EIT) Law in 2008 levelled the playing field for foreign and domestic business. Meanwhile, local administrations and investment zones have less authority to offer tax holidays (often up to three years) to attract foreign companies, with the exception of some high-tech investments.
- **High operating costs.** Multinational companies operating in China typically come under closer scrutiny than domestic players or their Hong Kong and Taiwanese counterparts. This means that western companies must ensure that

they maintain international standards in areas such as tax, labour, health and safety and broader compliance obligations.

◪ **Trade disputes.** Foreign companies can be hit hard by international trade disputes and intergovernment squabbles. Between 1979 and 2007, China faced nearly 600 charges of anti-dumping at a cost of more than $16 billion, exacerbating international tensions and prompting retaliatory measures, which upset trade relations. Multinationals will always be hostages to such trade disputes and are advised not to be drawn into discussions about foreign policy issues or intergovernmental tensions.

◪ **Quality fade.** Successful partnerships do not run themselves. The welcoming local partner whose innovative production methods can match the foreign investor's required specifications can also pose problems down the line. Having secured lucrative contracts or entered into beneficial partnerships with multinational companies, many local companies then turn their attention to cutting corners on the manufacturing process in a bid to drive down their own costs – often resorting to dangerous and illegal measures. Ingredients, components, processes and packaging may all be compromised, resulting in products that over time fall substantially below the quality standards agreed under the original terms of the partnership. Paul Midler, a businessman who has worked in China, describes this as "quality fade". Effective testing of China-made products by external test laboratories reduces the risk from this source.

◪ **Patchy enforcement.** Corporate headquarters should be aware that although the domestic competition may lack the efficiencies or production quality of multinational companies, they are often able to operate in a regulatory grey area either because they enjoy close links to local government officials or because they are rarely scrutinised by the local authorities to the same degree as their foreign counterparts.

◪ **Poor intellectual property protection.** Although China now has the full complement of laws to ensure intellectual property (IP) protection in theory, in practice this remains one of the biggest worries for foreign companies with Chinese operations. Enforcement agencies lack the teeth, profile and support to take on companies that violate IP legislation, particularly when those companies have strong connections to local government. China-based brand protection managers of European consumer-goods companies try not to inform the local police force when their team is about to raid a factory suspected of producing counterfeit goods because they know that the police may well warn the factory beforehand. Such collusion is typically found in villages and small towns outside the major cities where counterfeit operations can support entire districts or communities.

Table 1.3 **A comparative disadvantage balance sheet**

| China comparative disadvantage | Advantages for western firms |
|---|---|
| *Factors of production* | |
| Capital market inefficiency | Outperform in capital intensive sectors |
| The curse of labour | Greater flexibility of technology-intensive firms |
| Innovation gap | High returns to innovation |
| Environmental inefficiency | Opportunity for environment/resource-efficient products |
| *Legal/political systems* | |
| Governance technology | Faster standard and policy cycles |
| Competition policy | Superior responsiveness to consumer demand |
| Legal system weakness | Legal-intensive industries (eg, finance) |
| Political reform risk | Higher certainty in strategic planning |
| *Commercial issues* | |
| Margin compression in manufacturing | Higher returns to creativity |
| Slow to internationalise | Superior global brand management |
| Tax aversion/IT | Higher returns to IT |
| Undervalue intangibles | Better economies of scope |

Sources: *China Economic Quarterly; The Economist*

## Summary

- **If at first you don't succeed, keep trying.** Most successful companies have succeeded in China only through perseverance and learning from their mistakes.
- **There is no magic to *guanxi*.** It makes perfect sense to build corporate networks as a means of doing business in a society where relationships are so highly valued.
- **Manage corporate expectations early and effectively.** China-based managers need to manage the sometimes overblown expectations of head office early and effectively.

# 2 The political and economic context

A weak-willed person in the revolutionary ranks cannot stand the sugar-coated bullets of the bourgeoisie.

Chinese-English Dictionary published by the Beijing Foreign Languages Institute, 1979

China's leadership will not admit it, but it faces some of the greatest problems of any administration since the founding of the People's Republic of China in 1949. The enduring spectre of official corruption; a yawning income gap between urban haves and rural have-nots; the popularisation of communications technology such as mobile phones and the internet – all these serve to destabilise a political system that for more than 40 years ruled through communist ideology but since the collapse of the former Soviet Union has moved towards the pursuit of wealth. Yet at the same time, the collective ability of the leadership to handle these problems is also the greatest it has been since that date. Unlike their predecessors, today's leaders are younger, reform-minded and outward-looking (often overseas-educated), selected for their professional rather than their political credentials.

China's development may appear to be driven by economic forces. Yet since it took power, the ruling Communist Party of China (CPC) has used economic reforms to maintain social stability and strengthen its political monopoly, based on a Marxist-Leninist ideology. Over the past six decades, three pillars have supported the Chinese system: the party, the state and the army. The party decides policy; the state implements it; and the army enforces it. Although the three wield joint power, it is the party that dominates government.

## The party

With 72m members, the CPC is the world's largest political party. Its highest official body, the National People's Congress (NCP), serves as China's parliament with 3,000-odd delegates selected from local congresses representing the provinces, municipalities, autonomous regions and armed forces. The NPC is only just beginning to show signs of shrugging off its reputation as a rubber-stamp body, though this process is expected to take many years. At its annual session (typically in March), the NPC meets to approve long-term policy and revisions to the party constitution.

The NPC's Central Committee makes executive decisions when the NPC is not in session (which is most of the time). The Central Committee in turn selects the Politburo, a supreme policymaking body within which an even more elite group, the Standing Committee, sits. This small group of leaders, which currently comprises nine people, holds the real power.

Below the NPC, the CPC structure extends downwards to provincial, municipal, city, township and village levels, permeating every level of society through committees and local-level party cells, which operate in factories, urban neighbourhoods, villages and schools. Through these cells and committees the CPC is supposed to keep in touch with popular issues and concerns, shaping policy accordingly. In practice, the flow is usually one way – from the top down.

The cumulative impact of market reforms, improving lifestyles and communism's defeat elsewhere around the world has diminished the strength of CPC control. Many now see the party not as an ideological pillar but as a stepping-stone to a successful career. The party is the world's biggest business association, and membership can provide useful *guanxi* for ambitious executives. Even today, party members take the best jobs in government, academia, financial institutions and a host of other sectors.

## The state

China's vast state structure mirrors that of the CPC. At each level of government there is a people's (state) congress and a people's government. The country's administrative divisions comprise 22 provinces, four municipalities directly under central government control and five "autonomous regions" for some of China's 55 ethnic minorities. These autonomous regions are:

- south-western Guangxi, home to the Zhuang and dozens of other small minorities;
- Inner Mongolia (Nei Menggu), created in part from regions of former Manchuria allocated to China by the Soviet Union in 1947 after the second world war;
- north-western Ningxia, a small region on the old Silk Road trading route squeezed into the barren land between the Gobi desert and the Tibetan plateau, home to the Muslim Hui;
- Tibet (Xizang), with a population of 2.8m Tibetans;
- far-western Xinjiang, a predominantly Islamic region bordering Pakistan, Kazakhstan, Uzbekistan, a 50-mile Afghanistan corridor and southern Russia, where some 9m Uygurs, Kazakhs and a

sprinkling of Uzbeks and Tatars live (as well as more than 8m Han Chinese).

The autonomous regions function like the provinces but officially enjoy an additional mandate because of their cultural differences with the majority Han-Chinese population. In practice, Beijing controls these regions as rigorously as the provinces (if not more so) because of their ethnic minority populations and in some cases – notably Xinjiang and Tibet – their historically restive relations.

China's four municipalities – Beijing, Chongqing, Shanghai and Tianjin – enjoy the same political and economic status and responsibilities as the provinces and autonomous regions. Another nine – Chongqing, Dalian, Guangzhou, Harbin, Ningbo, Qingdao, Shenyang, Wuhan and Xi'an – have special economic autonomy. Beneath these is a hierarchy of prefectures, counties, cities, townships and villages, all of which answer to the level above. The government's ambitious urbanisation policy, which is expected to continue until 2020 when it is estimated that urban residents will outnumber the rural population, has seen city authority expand to include outlying rural districts, as the government seeks to develop infrastructure and raise incomes while strengthening the supply of raw materials and agricultural produce to the cities.

China has 651 cities, 113 of them with populations of more than 1m. The country's official urban population has risen from 20% in 1980 (a figure usually associated with some of the world's poorest countries) to 45% in 2007, or 594m out of the 1.32 billion total population. This figure is believed to be slightly exaggerated by definitions of administrative urban areas, but the achievement remains a remarkable one. China is aiming for a 70% urbanisation rate by 2030, putting it higher than Japan's current rate. It sees urbanisation as crucial to continued economic development and so is investing in the infrastructure required to accommodate 400m new city residents. A report published by the McKinsey Global Institute in 2008 predicts that by 2025 China will have 219 cities with more than 1m people and 24 with more than 5m.

## Controlling the economy

The 50-member State Council is the central government's "cabinet", the highest administrative government body in the country. Meeting once a month under the leadership of the premier, the State Council also has a Standing Committee comprising the CPC secretary-general, four vice-premiers and a number of ministers; it meets as often as twice weekly.

State Council members, including the premier, may serve a maximum of two consecutive five-year terms.

Reporting directly to the State Council are more than 20 government entities, most of which (with the notable exception of the Ministry of Finance) have been reformed, restructured and renamed over the past 30 years. The number of ministries has gradually fallen, with those responsible for the economy and industry going through several evolutionary cycles. The current Ministry of Commerce (Mofcom) was born out of the Ministry of Foreign Trade and Economic Co-operation (Moftec), previously known as the Ministry of Foreign Economic Relations and Trade (Mofert) – itself created from a merger of the old Ministry of Economic Relations with Foreign Countries and trade bureaux from other ministries, dating back to the Ministry of Foreign Trade (set up in 1952). Meanwhile, the current Ministry of Industry and Information Technologies (MIIT) supersedes the Ministry of Information Industry which itself was created from the Ministry of Posts & Telecommunications (MPT)

## The army

The third pillar of China's power is the People's Liberation Army (PLA). Many older Chinese have a special respect for the PLA because its revolutionary roots are intertwined with those of the party, while the younger generation is educated and provided with a regular supply of pro-army, nationalist propaganda. Images of soldiers heroically packing sandbags against flooding riverbanks flash across television screens every year. Over the past 20 years, steadily growing defence budgets have helped streamline and modernise the army immeasurably – a strategic decision taken following the mighty display of US military technology in the first Gulf war of 1990.

## Leadership by consensus, not individuals

Mao Zedong's leadership of the People's Republic of China (PRC) from 1949 until his death in 1976 continued a tradition of individual-led leadership passed on from the imperial tradition of previous dynasties. The CPC had fought a 28-year civil war that culminated in the retreat of Chiang Kai-Shek and the Chinese Nationalist Party (Kuomintang) to Taiwan. After gaining power in 1978, two years after his old rival Mao's death, Deng Xiaoping took over as undisputed leader (though he did not accept any formal positions), introducing economic reforms that heralded a fundamental economic transition.

Leadership successions are never comfortable in China, particularly in the era of consensus that the government has now entered. Political authority in China is personal, relying on individual relationships within the political structure that have been developed and nurtured for years. This personal network has traditionally rendered formal structures, organisations and procedures largely powerless, and explains why Deng Xiaoping was the most powerful person in China when his only official position was as chairman of the Beijing Bridge Association.

Since the political crisis that followed the Tian'anmen Square protests in 1989, consensus has become essential for the leadership to survive. The appointment of Jiang Zemin in 1989 initiated a gradual move towards more collective leadership, though his elevation was the result of intense backroom negotiations, political jockeying and compromise. With the death of the 92-year-old Deng in 1997, the generation of revolutionary leaders – and the link to the pre-1911 belief that the country's leader was somehow bequeathed with higher moral qualities – finally drew to a close.

### Elite groupings

The political elite is divided into groups that do not really qualify as "factions" but nonetheless help to make clear the political pressures at play:

*Tuanpai* – Hu-Wen's group, many members of which are his former Communist Youth League colleagues.

*Taizidang* ("Princelings") – children of CPC veterans.

*Shanghaibang* – Jiang Zemin's Shanghai faction has lost ground and is unlikely to regain influence.

Technocrats – not yet a true faction but an emerging grouping of specialists, mainly in the financial and economic bureaucracy.

### Hu and Wen

Consensus leadership has strengthened under Hu Jintao (born in December 1942), president and CPC secretary-general, following a smooth transfer of power to the "fourth generation" leadership in 2002–03, which became a second five-year term at the CPC Congress in late 2007. Hu is also state president and chairman of the Central Military Commission (CMC), the highest military body in the country and the outlet through which the PLA exercises its power at the highest level. Hu's right-hand man is Premier Wen Jiabao (born in September 1942), a political survivor who as head of the CPC General Office accompanied then CPC secretary general Zhao Ziyang (who died in 2005 after 16 years under house arrest) to Tian'anmen Square to try to persuade pro-democracy protesters to leave before the military crackdown in June 1989. (See Appendix 3 for a list of politburo standing committee members.)

### The next generation and the evolving CPC

The "fifth generation" of leaders who will succeed the Hu–Wen administration assumes power in 2012. Two key players have emerged. The first, Xi Jinping (born in June 1953), a former Shanghai party secretary who was promoted to the CPC politburo standing committee and the vice-presidency in 2008, is favourite to take over the CPC leadership from Hu at the Eighteenth Party Congress in 2012 when the latter's term expires. The second, Li Keqiang (born in July 1955), who studied law at Beijing University in 1978–82, was appointed vice-premier and elevated to the CPC politburo standing committee in 2008 and is expected to be named premier at the NPC annual session in March 2013.

When Mikhail Gorbachev, then president of the Soviet Union, visited Beijing in May 1989, student protesters in Tian'anmen Square commented ruefully that China's Gorbachev was "still in high school" – recognition of the fact that political reform clearly lay decades away. Yet if (as is likely) they are appointed, Xi and Li will be the youngest leaders to hold these positions in the history of the PRC. More significantly, they will be the first leaders not to have been named as successors by individual leaders (Hu was identified by Deng as a successor to Jiang Zemin, CPC secretary-general, as far back as the early 1990s). Although Li is widely regarded as Hu's protégé, the fact that Hu could not name Li as his successor and that both central and provincial officials assessed the candidates for leadership positions reflects the extent to which the CPC has matured in the wake of communism's collapse in eastern Europe. Consultation (carefully controlled as it doubtless was) represents at least a small step towards a more democratic process; and although the CPC is still many steps away from the democracy that China needs in the long-term, this is a clear sign that it is edging towards a more flexible institutional structure.

Stimulating domestic demand is a priority for Li Keqiang, who underlined its importance while still party secretary in Henan. Li, who took a doctorate in economics at Beijing University (1988–95), dismisses over-attention to GDP figures and believes economic growth should be measured in growth of disposable real income. Li is expected to act as a counterbalance to Xi, supported by an able upper echelon of leaders who are expected to include Wang Qishan (vice-premier), Bo Xilai (Chongqing party secretary) and Wang Yang (Guangdong party secretary). Indeed, even the sixth-generation leadership (due to assume power in 2017–18) already appears to have been selected: Hu Chuanhua (Hebei provincial governor) and Sun Zhengcai (agriculture minister) represent a factional compromise aimed at preventing potentially destabilising power struggles. This continuation of the collective leadership model, which has served China well since the death of Deng, raises possible concerns that the bold political, social and economic reforms that are likely to be required over the next ten years may prove hard to achieve. The CPC certainly appears set to remain in power for the foreseeable future, facing negligible opposition and coming down hard on any challenges to its authority.

### Continuing economic growth is key to the CPC's survival

In factional struggles within the CPC in the 1980s and 1990s, generally younger, reform-mind moderates were pitted against older, more conservative party ideologues. The core issue was initially whether or not to move from a command economy to one dictated (or even merely influenced) by market forces. However, as the benefits of market reforms to people's livelihood became more apparent, the argument shifted to how fast the pace of economic reform should be. This remains the main bone of contention today. China has continued to travel down the path of market reform to the point where those conservative elements that remain within the upper party leadership lack the credibility to present an effective opposition to this broad trend. However, this does not mean that party infighting cannot slow or even stop the progress of individual reforms. For instance, a measure to strengthen property rights was abandoned in early 2006 because left-wing conservatives argued that it would increase the divide between society's haves and have-nots. The deadline for the unification of tax rates for foreign and local companies was also repeatedly extended for several years before eventually being passed in 2007.

CPC leaders know that their continuing survival depends on their ability to deliver economic wealth to the population. This requires continuing liberalisation of the economy and stable, sustainable growth. Hundreds of millions of people may have benefited from the economic reforms launched at the end of the 1970s, but even more have seen little or no improvement in their daily lives and prospects. Recognising this and the potential danger to stability should this state of affairs not be addressed, the current administration has focused increasingly on "social harmony" – improving the lot of the 850m or so people living in the countryside. Introduced by Hu at the NPC's annual session in 2008, the social harmony policy appears to be more talk than walk, though it does build on policy changes that have taken place in recent years. These include the removal of personal income tax for all rural citizens earning a monthly salary of less than Rmb800 ($118), 30-year land-use rights for farmers and better cover under a steadily improving medical insurance policy. A report published in 2009 by Credit Lyonnais Securities Asia (CLSA), a brokerage and investment group, highlights how direct government subsidies to rural households have also been crucial in improving farmer productivity and their relative spending power.

The party will continue to evolve and grow as the largest political party in the world, thanks in part to its role as a networking tool for local businessmen. One of the CPC's most significant policy changes was Jiang's decision in 2001 to start to admit private businessmen and entrepreneurs, moving the party away from its ideological roots but broadening its appeal and recognising the inevitability of business–party links. By this time, party members were running an estimated 113,000 private companies, most of them established after the members had joined the CPC.

The CPC is in metamorphosis: many of its underlying values have been discredited, yet its ability to adapt suggests that, unlike in the former Soviet bloc, the party will survive. However, further political reform is likely to become imperative in a free-market economy that is giving greater economic independence to an urban middle class. This might be manifested in a more robust NPC or even in the eight so-called "democratic parties", the CPC's formal notional opposition, which currently serve as mere affiliates to the party. The latter possibility stems from the appointment of two leaders of "democracy parties" to ministerial positions. David Shambaugh, professor of political science and international affairs at George Washington University and a veteran China specialist, does not believe that the CPC is in danger of collapse in the medium term, but he can imagine some level of political pluralism as China moves towards what he refers to as an "eclectic state".

However, for the time being ordinary Chinese have no say whatsoever in high-level CPC positions. Members of the politburo and its standing committee, as well as provincial party secretaries, are all selected at party conclaves with no pretence of mass participation. Among the elite, little has changed since the early days of the PRC: China's top leaders are not beholden to public opinion, choosing to respond to it as a matter of choice or tactics.

## Ethnic tensions

China's majority Han ethnic group accounts for more than 92% of the national population. The remaining 8% (some 120m people) is made up of 55 ethnic minorities, some of whom – notably Tibetans, Uygurs and Mongolians – are extremely angry at what they see as the systematic destruction of their heritage by a dominant Han power intent on inflicting cultural assimilation through coercion. Inevitably, the regions of greatest sensitivity are China's border regions, a number of which (Tibet, Guangxi, Xinjiang, Mongolia) are classed as autonomous regions. In the most serious ethnic violence seen in the region for some years, roughly 200 people died in street fighting between Uygurs and Han Chinese in Urumqi, capital of Xinjiang, in July 2009.

## The spectre of social unrest

Popular discontent is not only ethnically motivated. Social triggers for unrest include:

- growing rural–urban income disparity;
- urban unemployment and increasing lay-offs caused by the economic crisis;
- widespread corruption manifested in the form of arbitrary levies, fines and illegal land seizures;
- forced relocation of urban residents to make way for new developments;
- failure to pay migrant workers in the cities;
- environmental pollution.

Data published by the Ministry of Public Security on "mass incidents" and "public order disturbances" showed a steady increase in unrest from the mid-1990s to the mid-2000s, with the number of mass incidents rising from 8,700 in 1993 to 87,000 in 2005. With no official data released since, it is difficult to assess whether public unrest has continued to grow, though unofficial estimates and anecdotal evidence would suggest it has. *Liaowang*, a magazine published by the state-controlled Xinhua news agency, reported that some 90,000 mass incidents occurred in 2006, and an annual publication by a state-backed academic institution reported that "more than 80,000" took place in 2007. There were believed to be over 127,000 protests (called "mass incidents" by the authorities) involving more than 12m people across the country in that year. Certainly, anecdotal evidence of labour unrest in the export-dependent regions of eastern

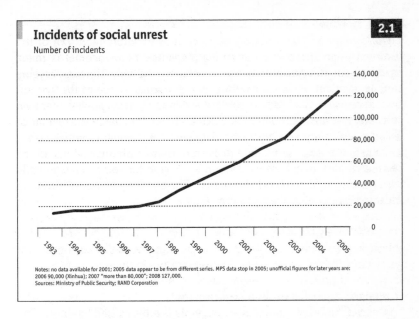

**Incidents of social unrest** 2.1
Number of incidents

Notes: no data available for 2001; 2005 data appear to be from different series. MPS data stop in 2005; unofficial figures for later years are: 2006 90,000 (Xinhua); 2007 "more than 80,000"; 2008 127,000.
Sources: Ministry of Public Security; RAND Corporation

and southern China in late 2008 suggests that labour unrest increased markedly in 2008. Andrew Gilholm, a Shanghai-based analyst at Control Risks, an international risk consultancy, points to the fact that tens of thousands of incidents of unrest have taken place each year over the past decade – in stark contrast to the popular image of a tightly controlled and ordered, submissive society.

Conditions in many factories in China can be difficult for workers. Workplace safety can be poor, for reasons that include overwork, poor training, exposure to hazardous materials and lack of appropriate working equipment and clothing. Although many foreign-invested enterprises (FIEs) ensure high standards in their own factories, some managers seek to cut overall operating costs, and so increase profitability or maintain competitiveness in an increasingly price-sensitive market, by making savings in areas that can affect working conditions. Foreign firms unwittingly increase their operating risks by subcontracting their operations to companies whose working culture places a lower priority on workers' rights and safety.

Migrant workers from other parts of China are an additional source of potential unrest for the authorities. China is experiencing one of the largest movements of people in world history, with more than 150m people living away from their officially registered place of residence in

2005 (compared with 131m in 2000). On the one hand, these migrants provide cheap labour in the big cities, while also remitting much-needed income back to their home villages in impoverished rural areas left behind in the largely urban economic boom. On the other hand, they are a highly mobile segment of the population living among communities that are benefiting from China's economic policies far more than the migrants themselves.[1] Migrant workers in the major cities are generally treated as second-class citizens by both their neighbours and local government.

Joblessness also raises risks of social unrest. China has experienced high unemployment before: in an unemployment spike in the late 1990s some 35m people lost their jobs. But at that time the jobless were mainly older workers being laid off from failing state-owned enterprises; the current wave affects both migrant workers who have already glimpsed the good life in the cities, and a generation of younger, better-educated job-seekers who have grown up with the economy going only one way – up. More than 4m college graduates enter the job market each year. In the event of protests, college graduates might be more likely to vent their frustration by staging co-ordinated protests.

Despite the likely increase in large-scale protests and the changing profile of protesters, disturbances are generally highly localised and do not yet pose a broader threat to central government. Jobless workers have neither the cohesion nor the inclination to unite broadly against the government. Co-ordinated protests remain unlikely.

## Social harmony

In 2006 the CPC Central Committee formally adopted Hu's proposal to "build a harmonious socialist society", seeking to place social concerns such as the yawning income gap between urban rich and rural poor, access to decent education and effective health care, endemic official corruption and environmental pollution on a par with economic growth.[2] Government spending on health, education, housing and social security increased in line with this initiative and was forecast to reach Rmb900 billion ($132 billion) in 2009, and a Rmb850 billion ($125 billion) health-care programme was rolled out in 2008–10. Yet China's wealth gap, broadly split between the haves in coastal provinces and the have-nots in central and western regions, is already at a critical level: China now has the highest relative income inequality in the region after Nepal, according to an UNCTAD report on least developed countries published in 2008.

Of equal concern to Beijing is the knowledge that the 20-year exodus of rural migrants that helped fuel economic development in coastal regions is beginning to ease. The combined effects of the global financial crisis, cost-cutting by manufacturers and gradually improving economic conditions at home have persuaded many migrant workers to return to their home towns and villages. This provided an unprecedented inflow of skilled workers to the provinces of Anhui and Henan, from which tens of millions of migrants left to work in the coastal cities in the 1980s and 1990s. Up to 20m migrant workers out of a total migrant population of 130m are believed to have lost their jobs in 2008, according to Khalid Malik, the UN Development Programme's China representative.

A factory manager based in Dongguan, a manufacturing centre in southern Guangdong province between the provincial capital Guangzhou and Shenzhen on the border with Hong Kong, estimates that more than one-third of all factories (typically involved in export-processing) in the area had been forced to close as a result of the global recession and tougher enforcement of safety policies in manufacturing. It remains to be seen what effect the reduction in migrant labour wages, which contributed nearly 40% to rural household incomes in 2008, will have on the rural population.

While economic growth generates the wealth required to address issues of social concern, one of Hu's biggest challenges is getting the support of local government officials for central directives on building a more stable, caring economic system as they have favoured rapid growth, believing it will help them gain promotion (and accumulate wealth). Social harmony initiatives have therefore been accompanied by a new series of anti-corruption drives targeting official corruption that has plagued the CPC since the launch of the open-door policy in 1979 (see Chapter 8).

Today's leaders have redirected China's economic development initiatives away from 1990s-style development at all costs (with a heavy focus on urban growth) and more towards rural income growth and the improvement of rural conditions. Hu's policy towards "people-centred" development was endorsed at the 16th Party Congress in November 2002. In this respect, economic policy is returning to the original model of the 1980s, where state support for rural development and entrepreneurialism contributed to an extraordinary improvement in the lives of the rural population.[3] Social performance is improving, initially with a modest decline in household educational expenditure. Hu's new policies – harmonious society, scientific development and energy efficiency – have already had a significant impact on the majority of (largely rural-based) Chinese, who have benefited little from market reforms.

In his political report to the 17th Party Congress in 2007, Hu emphasised that the government would focus on raising average household asset incomes – and in his speech he used the word "democracy" 61 times. The new direction for economic policy faces opposition from government officials and state-owned enterprise (SOE) managers who benefited from the 1990s model. Yet growing public resentment of what is widely seen as an overpowerful state sector is reflected in the (negative-sounding) term *guojin mintui* (the state advances, the private sector retreats), which some independent media claim has resulted in the misallocation of the lion's share of the $585 billion economic stimulus (intended to bring economic relief to all) going to SOEs. Despite the state's continuing control over the economy, the private sector has still grown massively, from 140,000 companies in 1992 to some 6.6m by the end of 2008.

### Public health care

Improvements in social harmony and scientific development are closely linked to public health care – a politically sensitive area for the authorities. Not only did the development-at-all-costs economic policy of the 1990s widen the income gap between (generally urban) rich and (generally rural) poor, but the market-oriented health reforms rolled out during the decade also accentuated the urban/rural difference in the quality of health-care provisions and fuelled widespread dissatisfaction among the rural population. After five years of planning, a new health-care reform plan was announced by the CPC Central Committee and State Council in 2009, along with a pledge of Rmb850 billion ($125 billion) in support, Rmb331 ($49 billion) of which will come from central government.

The health-care plan, which sets initial goals to provide basic health care to every urban and rural citizen by 2011 and a comprehensive system by 2020, reflects the new direction of the Hu–Wen leadership in seeking to address urban/rural inequalities through the policies of social harmony and scientific development. Under the scheme, the annual insurance premium for rural residents (up to 91.5% of the rural population in 2009) rose initially to Rmb150 ($22) in 2010, with the state paying 80% of this. Key elements of the plan serve as a reminder of the move away from the market and towards public welfare: "zero-profit system for medication sales".

More effective, farther-reaching health care is needed more than ever. The risk of widespread outbreaks of diseases is significant in China. Its large and increasingly mobile populations were vulnerable to the highly infectious severe acute respiratory syndrome (SARS), which severely disrupted business in 2003 and exposed the shortcomings of the rural

Table 2.1 **Selected economic indicators**

|  | 2004 | 2005 | 2006 | 2007 | 2008 | 2009 |
|---|---|---|---|---|---|---|
| GDP (% real change) | 10.08 | 10.43 | 11.60 | 13.00 | 9.00 | |
| Real agriculture (Rmb bn) | 1,642 | 1,727 | 1,814 | 1,881 | 1,984 | |
| Real industry (Rmb bn) | 6,818 | 7,616 | 8,606 | 9,871 | 10,789 | |
| Real services (Rmb bn) | 4,631 | 5,117 | 5,736 | 6,528 | 7,148 | |
| Agriculture (% real change) | 6.3 | 5.20 | 5.00 | 3.70 | 5.50 | |
| Industry (% real change) | 11.1 | 11.70 | 13.00 | 14.70 | 9.30 | |
| Services (% real change) | 10.0 | 10.50 | 12.10 | 13.80 | 9.50 | |
| Consumer prices (% change, average) | 3.85 | 1.77 | 1.76 | 4.77 | 5.90 | |
| Exchange rate (average, Rmb/$) | 8.28 | 8.19 | 7.97 | 7.61 | 6.95 | |
| Inward direct investment ($bn) | 54.94 | 79.13 | 78.10 | 138.41[a] | 147.79[a] | |
| Outward direct investment ($bn) | –1.81 | –11.31 | –21.16 | –17.00[a] | –53.47[a] | |
| Population aged 0–14 (%) | 22.27 | 21.37 | 20.85 | 20.44 | 20.10 | |
| Population aged 15–64 (%) | 70.26 | 71.03 | 71.42 | 71.69 | 71.92 | |
| Population aged 65+ (%) | 7.47 | 7.60 | 7.74 | 7.87 | 7.98 | |

a Estimate.
Sources: Economist Intelligence Unit, CountryData; Market Indicators and Forecasts

health-care system (poor reporting lines and inadequate health-care provisions), causing public anger at the cost of medical treatment. Furthermore, the density of humans and animals in close contact with each other in rural communities in southern China encourages the spread of viruses such as avian influenza (bird flu) and H1N1 swine flu.

State health-care policy will take time to implement and take effect. Pandemics and localised outbreaks of disease pose threats to business, particularly to multinational businesses with far-reaching supply chains and a growing reliance on China as both producer and consumer.

Chapter 3 discusses how investors can best prepare themselves for pandemic and other health risks.

## The economic environment

In the space of three decades, China has transformed an inward-looking, planned economy into a diversified, export-oriented system driven largely by market forces. When Deng opened the country's doors to foreign investment in 1979, import and export volumes accounted for less than 10% of GDP; by 2008, they accounted for 70%. By the end of 2008, the number of foreign-invested enterprises or FIEs (companies wholly or partly owned by foreign investors) in China had grown to 435,000. Even by 1995, FIEs controlled more than half China's exports, far more than the 25% controlled by foreign companies in South Korea at the height of its export-processing period in the second half of the 1970s. China is unique in having received unprecedented levels of labour-intensive and export-focused foreign direct investment (FDI). It is now the world's third largest economy behind the United States and Japan, ahead of Germany, the UK and France, and the second largest economy behind the United States based on purchasing power parity. In early 2009 Ting Lu, a China economist at Merrill Lynch, an investment bank, projected that China would overtake Japan in "three to four years". China's daily GDP in 2008 was more than its annual GDP for 1953.

### History of modern China's economic structure
#### 1950s and 1960s: going it alone
In 1949 the CPC's chief goal was to develop China into a modern and powerful industrial state. The economy lay in ruins after almost ten years of Japanese occupation and nearly three decades of civil war. In the 1950s, the former Soviet Union was China's only significant source of financial assistance, and the CPC's economic development policy followed that of the Soviet Union: a centrally planned command economy dominated by heavy industry. Based on the Soviet model, China's first five-year plan in 1953 marked its own attempt at rapid industrialisation. Initial results were inspiring: by 1957, the industrial sector was at least three times larger than in 1952.

Before the second world war agricultural production had accounted for almost two-thirds of China's national income. Yet as the industrial sector grew and the population soared, the agriculture sector started to fall behind; in 1957, grain production increased by just 1%. Mao opted for a collectivisation of agriculture along Soviet lines, arguing that this would allow the government to control grain prices and so generate the capital required to help fuel industrial growth. Moderates within the party leadership, led by Liu Shaoqi,[4] a CPC politburo member, argued instead that any change in the agriculture sector should be gradual and should follow industrial development, which would be able to provide the machinery needed to improve the means of agricultural production. Nonetheless, Mao pushed ahead with a policy of self-reliance[5] and collectivisation of the peasantry.[6] Agricultural production was further undermined by the withdrawal of all Soviet technical assistance following the Sino-Soviet split in 1956 and Mao's subsequent decision to push ahead alone with the hugely ambitious task of achieving rapid industrialisation, while at the same time continuing to feed the country's ballooning population.[7] The catastrophic "Great Leap Forward" (1958–61) that followed led to one of the greatest famines in modern history and allowed Liu to reintroduce more rational economic policies based on supply and demand.[8]

Mao's return to political dominance in the run-up to the Cultural Revolution (1966–76) brought an end to Liu's economic reconstruction, eradicating all market-based policies and reimposing the policy of self-reliance. However, by the end of the 1960s a more moderate economic policy began to emerge through the influence of Premier Zhou Enlai. As Mao became increasingly incapacitated by Parkinson's disease, the emphasis shifted once again from self-reliance towards engagement with the outside world. Desperate for foreign technology as a means to rebuild its economy, China began to engage with Soviet-bloc states, as well as Japan. In 1972, China bought its first shipment of US wheat to supplement falling grain production at home. In 1973, it signed a $290m contract with Pullman Kellogg of the United States for the construction of 16 urea-ammonia plants to create essential chemical fertiliser for local agricultural production. The same year, China became an oil exporter, selling crude to Japan.

### 1970s and 1980s: opening the doors to foreign investment

Mao died in 1976. The "Gang of Four", which had taken advantage of Mao's deteriorating condition to seize power in the latter years of the Cultural Revolution, were arrested a month after his death, marking the official end of this turbulent decade and prompting a rare display of public celebration. Deng Xiaoping, first rehabilitated by Zhou Enlai in 1973 but purged once more in 1976 by the Gang of Four, was rehabilitated for a second time in 1977. The following year, China announced that it would accept foreign investment in the form of joint-equity ventures. During the course of 1979 a new economic plan emerged calling for a three-year period of "readjustment, restructuring, consolidation and improvement", driven by two young reformist protégés of Deng: Zhao Ziyang as premier, and Hu Yaobang as CPC secretary-general.

During the 1980s, economic reforms grew as the government gained confidence with the idea of investment from overseas – the lion's share coming from neighbouring Hong Kong as manufacturers moved their operations across the border into southern Guangdong province in search of cheap land and labour. The country's first zones were created in Guangdong and neighbouring Fujian province in 1984 in recognition of the central role played by overseas Chinese investors in economic development. The first four special economic zones (SEZs) were Shenzhen for Hong Kong, Zhuhai for Macau, Shantou for the Chaozhou area of north-eastern Guangdong and Xiamen for Taiwanese investors across the strait (see Chapter 3, pages 00–00).

As well as the SEZs, a series of policies easing investment restrictions and devolving power to local government and state enterprise sparked a surge in foreign investment, capital construction and domestic production. However, development of the country's infrastructure lagged behind growth, causing severe shortages and bottlenecks. The record trade deficit and general overheating of 1984–85 forced the government to put the entire economic reform programme into low gear. The overhaul of the price system took a back seat to the fight against inflation and renewed crackdowns on official corruption. Conservatives regained the upper hand for a short period, but by 1987 economic growth was at full throttle once again with continued reforms in areas such as the contract system (where individual workers or enterprises were given targets with payments linked to contract fulfilment) – a far cry from the "iron rice bowl" system that guaranteed wages and welfare for life. Property reform in 1987 allowed individuals to buy and sell the right to use land for a period of up to 30 years – a further incentive to invest longer-term in agricultural production.

Deng continued to drive the "grand international cycle" as the primary means of stimulating economic growth, using his lieutenants Zhao and Hu to support the policy and chivvy along coastal areas in the vanguard of the process. The emphasis on using cheap labour as a resource represented a sensitive political point for the government, which in previous decades would have complained about the exploitation of Chinese workers. In late 1988 conservative pressure to tighten central government control over the economy began to increase markedly, forcing credit to dry up in SOEs and foreign-invested businesses alike. The brutal crackdown on the student-led pro-democracy movement in June 1989 – which began as a much broader public demonstration against official corruption – and the subsequent ousting of Zhao and other reformists, further complicated China's economic problems. Foreign investment plummeted in the aftermath of Tian'anmen, while restrictive economic policies put in place by conservative leaders curbed demand but led to massive oversupply and rising unemployment. China's GDP in 1989 reached just 3.9% compared with 10.8% in 1988 – the lowest growth rate since 1978.

## 1990s and 2000s: development at all costs

Multinational companies slowly began to return to China in the 1990s, though restrictive policies by resurgent conservatives within the leadership under Premier Li Peng were holding back this recovery. In 1992 the 87-year-old Deng reinvigorated reforms with a much-publicised visit to southern China, where he praised development in the Shenzhen and Zhuhai SEZs. Provincial administrations were only too happy to kick-start the reform process once again, expanding investments and furthering reform. By 1993, China had become the world's second-largest recipient of FDI – a position it still holds. More companies were listed on China's two fledgling stock exchanges, in Shenzhen and Shanghai, and the property market embarked on an unprecedented boom as speculative money poured in. Pudong New Area, an investment zone set up in Shanghai in 1992 as a designated financial hub, began to grow in the spirit of "build it and they will come".

The economy started to overheat in 1993, with inflation re-emerging as the leadership's top concern. Premier Zhu Rongji's austerity campaign in 1994 slowed economic growth by tightening credit but failed to address emerging problems of unequal economic development between the western and eastern provinces, growing state-enterprise debt and a spiralling migrant population. After another short slowdown during which the economy caught its breath, growth resumed until the Asian financial crisis of 1997–98 prompted a collapse in other markets in the region and slowed the growth of China's economy as regional FDI dried up. China's economy remained largely protected from the worst effects of the "Asian contagion" in part because its banking sector had not become too integrated with the international banking system. To make up for the drop in FDI, the government embarked on an unprecedented spending campaign and encouraged ever-larger foreign investment projects – notably Shanghai GM, the US manufacturer's $1 billion joint venture with Shanghai Automotive Industry Corporation (SAIC), which saw the first Chinese-made Buick roll off the assembly line in 1998, a year after Shanghai GM was established.

China pulled through the end of the decade with little interruption to its economic development, which went into overdrive following the country's long-delayed accession to the World Trade Organisation in December 2001. This marked China's official arrival in the world trading community, a move that has irreversibly altered both China's economy and the world economic system. FDI levels accelerated through to 2005, followed by another surge in 2007–08, with utilised FDI reaching a record $92.4 billion in 2008.

## (Re)balancing act

The transition from command economy to market economy has transformed the lives of hundreds of millions of people in coastal provinces as FDI and heavy state spending have fuelled growth. Shanghai symbolised the development-at-all-costs model of economic growth of the 1990s. The city amassed vast wealth in a policy that has received some criticism for its anti-rural bias and for what Huang Yasheng, professor of political economy and international management at Sloan School of Management, calls "repression of small-scale and labour-intensive entrepreneurship". The Pudong project in particular had a profound impact on other local governments, which sought to emulate it in their own localities, contributing to land grabs across the country.

Yet the Shanghai model has been phenomenally expensive, having sucked in much of the state investment (and subsequently FDI) that could have gone to other parts of the country. The Maglev train, for example, which is prohibitively expensive to use and provides little practical help in getting to or from Shanghai's Pudong International Airport, will take at least 160 years to recoup the initial investment, according to an estimate by HSBC economists Qu Hongbin and Sophia Ma Xiaoping in 2006. Shanghai has been described as a "Potemkin" (apparently after Russian minister Grigory Potyomkin, leader of the Crimean military campaign, who in 1787 ordered the construction of façades of villages on the desolate banks of the River Dnieper in order to trick the visiting Empress Catherine into believing that Russia had conquered valuable towns and communities and so win favour with her).[9]

Regional growth campaigns such as "Develop the West" and "Revitalise the North-east" symbolise government efforts which to date have enjoyed only modest success with multinationals. Those foreign companies that relocated were drawn either by the region's natural resources (as in the case of Royal Dutch Shell) or by obligatory joint-venture partnerships, such as Ford Mazda's joint venture with Chang'an Automotive Group in Chongqing, where it has two plants (see Chapter 3). Yet after nearly a decade of heavy state spending, market forces are beginning to have an impact in the central and western regions. Growth is gradually shifting away from the coast as manufacturing costs rise and infrastructure links inland continue to improve, so encouraging more foreign investors to relocate. Unilever's manufacturing centre for detergents and personal care products in Hefei (capital of Anhui province) is one of the company's largest sites in the world. Global brands Siemens and Hitachi have operations in neighbouring Wuhu city.

As manufacturers move west, they are also benefiting from aspects of Mao's legacy, such as his "third-front" policies, which called for China's scientific base to be developed hundreds of miles inland, away from the enemy's bomber aircraft. Thus it is that inland cities such as Chengdu and Xi'an are home to a skilled workforce of highly affordable scientists and graduates. Intel, a US chipmaker, set up an operation in Chengdu in 2005.

## China's stockmarket

China's foray into the world of shares trading dates back to 1986, when prices were marked up in chalk on blackboards in chaotic exchanges in Shanghai and Shenyang. Four years later, two stock exchanges were formally established in Shanghai and Shenzhen, rapidly growing to become significant contributors to the government's fiscal revenues and an important source of financing for the state sector. In 1997 the CPC named the stockmarket as "an important component of the national economy" at its 15th congress. Yet a four-year slump from 2001 to 2005 wiped half of the value off the Shanghai market, ending only when the China Securities Regulatory Commission decided to float more than $200 billion in previously non-traded state-owned equity. This influx of millions of shares – along with the removal of a source of uncertainty in the form of state ownership – encouraged small-time investors to have a flutter on the market, causing another bull run that boosted the number of investors on the Shanghai Stock Exchange from 38m in 2004 to 41m in 2006.

Throughout its existence, the market has been a roller-coaster ride for local punters. But has it now left behind the days of *chao gupiao* ("stir-fried shares")? The central government hopes so. In the meantime, the long-awaited second board, the ChiNext stockmarket, opened in Shenzhen in late 2009 with a modest 28 listings: 25 private firms, two state-owned firms and one FIE. Modelled on New York's NASDAQ and London's AIM, ChiNext hoped to list 100 small and medium-sized enterprises (SMEs) in 2010. The government hopes, perhaps a little optimistically, that ChiNext will contribute much of the capital required by new companies as well as serving as part of an investment strategy for private equity investors looking for lucrative (and legal) exits from mainland investments.

## Who's who in China's financial sector
### The regulators
☑ People's Bank of China. Designated as the country's central bank in 1979, the PBOC is responsible for setting monetary policy and ensuring the stability of the

financial system. Over the past 30 years it has shed a number of other roles that were deemed to be in conflict with these core functions: in the 1990s, it handed over its responsibilities for supervising the securities and insurance sectors to the China Securities Regulatory Commission (CSRC) and the China Insurance Regulatory Commission (CIRC) respectively; and in 2003, it transferred its bank regulatory functions to the newly set up China Banking Regulatory Commission (CBRC). In return, the PBOC has taken on the job of fighting money-laundering and running the interbank bond market, which came into being in 2005.

- ☑ Ministry of Finance. The MOF, which began life in the early days of the PRC as a tax collector to finance government spending, is now responsible for China's fiscal affairs, such as controlling the national budget and raising finance from capital markets. The MOF no longer has sole ownership of the state's commercial and policy banks, though it retains a stake in most financial institutions.
- ☑ China Banking Regulatory Commission. Set up in 2003 to take over bank regulatory functions from the PBOC, the CBRC oversees nearly 9,000 institutions and some 2.7m bank staff. A growing responsibility is risk management and corporate governance, particularly with regard to fraud and malpractice by senior management in the state banks. A significant part of this involves the enforcement of Chinese accounting standards (similar to International Financial Reporting Standards or IFRS). Unlike other regulators, the CBRC falls under the control of the State Council and so lacks the independence of some other regulatory bodies.
- ☑ China Securities Regulatory Commission. Set up in 1992 following a series of market scandals involving local securities houses, the CSRC has sole responsibility for supervising China's securities and futures markets. Again, its main focus is on transparency and ethical practices within these once poorly controlled markets.
- ☑ China Insurance Regulatory Commission. The CIRC was spun off from the PBOC in 1998. Its function is to supervise and develop China's insurance industry: non-life, life and reinsurance.

### The players
- ☑ Big four state-owned commercial banks. These are Bank of China (BOC), China Construction Bank (CCB), Industrial and Commercial Bank of China (ICBC) and Agricultural Bank of China (ABC). The big four have transferred their non-performing loans to asset-management companies managed by the state. The BOC, CCB and ICBC are all listed on the Hong Kong or Shanghai stockmarkets, with the ABC scheduled to follow.
- ☑ Shareholding banks. There are 13 shareholding banks (also called joint-stock commercial banks) in which the state often holds a stake. These have generally

performed strongly, benefiting from strategic investors to help amass capital and improve transparency. They include Bank of Communications (BoCom), China Merchants Bank (CMB), CITIC Bank, China Minsheng Banking Corp, Shanghai Pudong Development Bank (SPDB), Industrial Bank, China Everbright Bank (CEB), Huaxia Bank, Guangdong Development Bank (GDB), Shenzhen Development Bank (SDB), Hengfeng Bank, Zheshang Bank and China Bohai Bank.

◪ City, regional and rural commercial banks. There are some 125 city commercial banks.

## The global financial crisis
### Triple whammy
The global financial crisis of late 2008 was the last of three blows to China's economy between 2006 and 2008. The first was in 2006–07, when the economy began to encounter problems arising from the inevitable increase in land and labour costs in southern and eastern China as economic development reduced these regions' competitiveness. At the same time, a series of high-profile product and food-safety scandals caused public outrage and led to tougher manufacturing regulations, forcing thousands of businesses to shut down, particularly in southern China. The second was the collapse of the property market in December 2007 – with pre-Olympic Beijing at the centre of an unprecedented construction programme – which slashed demand for heavy industrial materials and sent shockwaves down the manufacturing chain. Jack Rodman of Global Distressed Solutions, a Beijing-based property specialist, estimates that some 500m sq. feet of commercial property was developed in Beijing between 2006 and 2008 – more than all the office space in Manhattan – and that was excluding government projects. By the end of 2008 some 20% of this space was unoccupied.

### Export worries
The onset of the global financial crisis sent China's exports into freefall. Initial indications supported a popular perception that China's economy would remain largely insulated from the worst effects of the economic crisis, since exports comprised a comparatively small part (perhaps 20%) of the overall economy. However, the fall in exports also meant a fall in imports (of raw materials and goods used to manufacture products for export), which led to more closures of both domestic and foreign-invested manufacturing plants.

By early 2009, as a result of rising costs and tougher product safety regulations, up to 40% of factories situated in the southern industrial belt that stretches from Guangzhou southwards to Hong Kong were thought to have closed, pushing an estimated 20m migrant workers into joblessness. Global accounting firm PricewaterhouseCoopers estimated that 670,000 small firms had already closed across China by early 2009 as a consequence of the financial crisis. (China has an estimated 7m companies.) It was initially feared that bankruptcies of small businesses too small to cope with the downturn and credit crisis could break up the links in China's supply chain and so undermine the country's export economy. This fear has now passed as economic recovery has continued, but it is likely to be several years before export demand reaches pre-downturn levels.

### Stimulus package

In late 2008 the Chinese government announced a massive two-year Rmb4 trillion ($588 billion) stimulus package to support the economy. Fuelled by massive bank lending, this had some success in supporting growth, though not without concerns. First, the actual amount of the package was some $180 billion, since much of the money promised was already part of existing stimulus packages intended for infrastructure spending. Second, the initial effects of the stimulus benefited mainly major cities and coastal provinces rather than the central and western regions, which have seen less development.

To stimulate economic growth the government also spent an unprecedented $1.7 trillion in the first three quarters of 2009 alone – 136% more than in the same period in 2008 – mainly in infrastructure, manufacturing and property. Thanks in large part to stimulus efforts, the economy was expected to exceed the 8% growth target set by Premier Wen as *bao ba*, or "protecting eight [%]" in 2010. Chinese policymakers adhere to the 8% figure as the minimum growth threshold needed to create enough jobs for the country's enormous population, though there is no evidence to support this. It is more likely that the official media sticks to this number because of its traditional association with wealth and prosperity (*ba* sounds likes *fa*, to prosper).

### A growing role in the global economy

From a domestic perspective China is in a stronger credit and fiscal position than virtually any other major economy. Total official government debt, including the informal borrowings of local governments, is thought to be around 20% of GDP, thanks to what Arthur Kroeber, managing editor of

*China Economic Quarterly*, calls a "sensible counter-cyclical fiscal policy" that allows scope for sustained fiscal expansion. (Fitch Ratings estimates that the government's debts by the end of 2008 represented 21.8% of the country's GDP.) Strong fiscal accounts give China the ability to sustain its stimulus programme – one of the world's largest such programmes, equivalent to 10–12% of GDP – through 2010.

Meanwhile, Chinese banks have now officially lowered their non-performing loan (NPL) ratios to just 2% of assets – albeit by simply removing NPLs from the books and handing them over to specially created "asset management corporations" to sell off the debt. They also have strong capital ratios (above 10% at most banks) and high required reserve ratios of around 15%, enabling them to unlock funds as and when necessary. China's economic health contrasts with ailing debt-ridden economies in other parts of the world, and puts it in a position to play a stabilising role in the new global financial order, according to a report published at the end of 2008 by the Deloitte China Research and Insight Centre, part of Deloitte Touche Tohmatsu, a global accounting firm.

## Recurrent risks

### Inflation
Fluctuations in international oil prices can affect inflation for short periods, but structural issues – such as the decade-long urban construction boom which ended China's last deflationary cycle in the late 1990s – can place enormous demand pressures on raw materials and intermediate products. Other structural challenges include energy demand, as China is producing massive amounts of energy-intensive products such as aluminium, cement and steel; currency appreciation; and the new labour law, which requires businesses to offer permanent employment to workers with more than ten years of employment.

### Exchange rate
Exchange rate risk is an increasingly important factor for companies involved in international trade in China. Given the nascent state of currency hedging in China, it is possible that many firms, especially local ones, could face problems if the renminbi's value against other currencies fluctuates substantially.[10] This could lead the government to take unforeseen measures to shore up the trading sector. Companies should ensure that both they and any Chinese firms they have contractual relations with (such as suppliers) are properly protected against possible movements in the exchange rate. In 2008 the government moved to tighten controls

on foreign exchange through stricter monitoring of trade-related foreign-exchange flows, in order to prevent this being used for speculation on renminbi appreciation, causing expensive delays for traders. Inflows of hot money appeared to reverse in the second half of 2008, but if they escalated again further measures could be introduced, whose effect would be to increase paperwork and delays for those who make regular foreign currency transactions.

### Damaged trust

The trust that Chinese companies and the government placed in the stability of foreign financial firms and manufacturers has been badly dented by the global financial crisis. In the wake of the crisis, foreign companies doing business with China may find that local suppliers are less confident of assurances of financial stability from their foreign partners. Chinese companies may gain little reassurance from legal safeguards since many will be loath to pursue cases abroad against companies that breach contract terms or go bankrupt. Foreign investors may have to provide higher deposits, upfront payments, references from trusted parties or other guarantees. At the same time, foreign companies should bear in mind that Chinese partners may be experiencing difficulties because of similar crisis-induced economic pressures.

### From investment to consumption: don't hold your breath

China's economic development has been fuelled in part by constant and increasingly substantial FDI inflows, accompanied by unprecedented state investment in infrastructure. But when will the Chinese economy reach the point where it moves from an investment-fuelled, export-driven economy to one characterised by domestic consumption? Many observers believe that point has already come, pointing to retail sales data demonstrating domestic spending that rivals US consumption.

This is a somewhat optimistic view. The entry point for households in this consumption bracket is estimated at $5,000 a year. Roughly 90% of Chinese households spend less than this, using their money for subsistence items: food, clothes and housing. Government officials have encouraged urbanisation in the belief that urban households earn more and so ultimately will consume more. Kroeber is "profoundly sceptical" of the exaggerated claims made for the consumer power of China's middle-income consumers. Most of the middle-income households with annual expenditure above $5,000 are in the three coastal regions surrounding the mega-cities of Beijing, Shanghai and Guangzhou/Shenzhen (the Bohai

Rim, Yangtze River Delta and Pearl River Delta respectively). Yet even in these regions the concentration of such households is not sufficient to justify a sales and distribution presence for some products and services. Multinational fast-moving consumer goods firms are thought to require a concentration of at least 200,000 consumption households in order to establish a viable market, according to MasterCard. Furthermore, as Kroeber says, "simply moving a farmer into a factory does not make him an economically significant consumer".

The ability to reach such a concentration will also require further heavy investment in China's transport system and continuing improvements in the country's evolving distribution and logistics capabilities. Logistics costs currently account for 20% of average goods prices in China compared with 10% in the United States, according to the US Department of Commerce. Lastly, the absence of adequate welfare structures to provide health care, education and unemployment support has obliged consumers to save (to pay for schooling or guard against sickness, old age or unemployment) rather than spend disposable income on consumer goods. Eventually China's per-head incomes will reach a level and scale where domestic consumption does play a dominant role in the economy, but this is likely to be many years away.

## Summary

- **Political stability will continue.** Political wrangling between reformists and conservatives in the upper echelons of the party leadership sometimes leads to hold-ups in policies affecting foreign investment. Foreign investors should be prepared for long delays in the introduction of key reforms. The government will only approve new laws or changes to existing laws when it is politically or economically expedient to do so.
- **Social stability. China** has seen an increase in social unrest over the past five years, sparked by official corruption, environmental disasters, relocation of communities, food and product safety scandals and a host of other worrying issues. Social stability remains the leadership's biggest challenge.
- **Economic strategy.** China emerged from the financial crisis in far better shape than most western governments, helped by a massive government stimulus programme. The emergence of a middle-income consumer segment is helping to boost domestic demand, but China's economy will continue to rely on heavy investment for many years.

# 3 Assessing the market: pre-market entry

There is nothing mysterious about China once you understand her.

Premier Zhou Enlai in conversation with Henry Kissinger, then US national security adviser

This chapter focuses on how investors should assess the market for their goods and services. It includes an analysis of the Chinese consumer and the most promising geographical markets for investment, including investment zones. It profiles the country's transport and logistics environment and offers strategies for distribution. It concludes with tips on market research and business intelligence.

## Getting to know the Chinese consumer

Before entering the China market it is essential to be clear about your aims, and therefore your needs. Are you seeking to establish a manufacturing business with an export-driven strategy, or one that focuses on the local consumer? Are you looking to sell to middle-class consumers in and around the wealthy cities of the coastal provinces, or to distribute mass products to both urban and rural consumers across the country?

To get a clearer idea of the market it helps to think of China as a patchwork of markets with all the variety of the European Union: culture, language, business practice, operating cost and consumer income and behaviour can vary hugely from region to region. Cities and their populations are changing at a bewildering speed, affecting all these categories. The emergence of a middle class and China's growing integration with global consumer trends has seen the emergence of a younger generation who share more similarities with their Asian (and global) counterparts through popular culture than any other consumer segment in the country's history.

The mass market comprises urban "blue-collar" workers who make up the majority of populations in the second- and third-tier cities that remain industrial centres. China's largest cities have seen an outflow of industry over the past five years. The most notable examples are Beijing, which moved its industry out of the city in preparation for hosting the Olympic Games in 2008, Shanghai, which did the same (though there was less to move) for the 2010 World Expo, and Guangzhou, which hosted the Asian

Table 3.1 **Growth in population, literacy and consumer prices**

|  | Population (m) | Adult literacy rate (% of pop. over 15) | Consumer prices (% change per year; average) |
|---|---|---|---|
| 1985 | 1,058.51 | – | 9.47 |
| 1986 | 1,075.07 | – | 5.73 |
| 1987 | 1,093.00 | – | 7.13 |
| 1988 | 1,110.26 | – | 18.86 |
| 1989 | 1,127.04 | – | 18.30 |
| 1990 | 1,143.33 | 77.00 | 3.10 |
| 1991 | 1,158.23 | 77.80 | 3.49 |
| 1992 | 1,171.71 | 78.60 | 6.40 |
| 1993 | 1,185.17 | 79.40 | 14.56 |
| 1994 | 1,198.50 | 80.10 | 24.25 |
| 1995 | 1,211.21 | 80.80 | 16.78 |
| 1996 | 1,223.89 | 81.50 | 8.30 |
| 1997 | 1,236.26 | 83.20 | 2.79 |
| 1998 | 1,247.61 | 83.80 | −0.77 |
| 1999 | 1,257.86 | 84.50 | −1.46 |
| 2000 | 1,267.43 | 85.20 | 0.34 |
| 2001 | 1,276.27 | 85.80 | 0.71 |
| 2002 | 1,284.53 | – | −0.75 |
| 2003 | 1,292.27 | – | 1.11 |
| 2004 | 1,299.88 | 90.90 | 3.85 |
| 2005 | 1,307.56 | – | 1.77 |
| 2006 | 1,314.48 | 90.9a | 1.76 |
| 2007 | 1,321.29 | – | 4.77 |
| 2008 | 1,328.02 | – | 5.90 |

Sources: Economist Intelligence Unit CountryData; Economist Intelligence Unit Market Indicators and Forecasts

Games in 2010. This exodus follows the gradual dismantlement of loss-making state-owned enterprises and the consequent lay-offs of tens of millions of state-sector workers across the country, followed by a surge in the number of smaller private and foreign-invested enterprises which have brought wealth to a growing section of the urban population.

## A growing middle class

China's middle-income consumer segment is the target for foreign-invested products and services. Definitions of what constitutes the Chinese middle-class consumer vary wildly, putting its size at anything from 50m people to as many as 400m. Is it an annual income of $3,000, $10,000, $20,000, or a combined household income of more than 2.5 times the average wage? Whatever the total estimate, this market segment is growing steadily in all the country's major cities, the greatest concentration being in coastal provinces and the development areas of the Yangtze River Delta around Shanghai, the Beijing-Tianjin corridor to the north and the Pearl River Delta with its hubs of Guangzhou and Shenzhen.

This fast-growing, youthful middle class has expectations and aspirations that broadly match its counterparts in other emerging markets. Middle-income consumers can afford to look beyond mass-market products to quality offerings from recognised local and foreign brands. Teenage students love fashion, music and consumer electronics, buying adidas shoes and Samsung phones; 20-something professionals eat at Pizza Hut and Häagen-Dazs (which has opened retail outlets in China) and make calls on iPhones; young families buy Volkswagen cars, Sony computers, Canon cameras and Pampers nappies.

Middle-class consumers have unprecedented access to events in China and across the globe through domestic and foreign media, though a carefully controlled educational curriculum and persisting social conventions exert a strong nationalist influence on their opinions – if not their choice of preferred brands. Yet unlike their comparatively jaded western counterparts, Chinese consumers are more receptive to branded content, says Ian Maskell, who over the course of more than a decade in China ran businesses for US confectionery giant Mars and Anglo-Dutch consumer goods company Unilever – if only because these concepts are a relative novelty.

## We may be nationalist – but we love foreign brands ...

Brands give consumers the chance to talk about themselves without speaking a word. Bergstrom Trends, a research consultancy that reports on

Table 3.2 **Where Chinese people work, m**

| | 2003 | 2004 | 2005 | 2006 | 2007 | 2008 |
|---|---|---|---|---|---|---|
| Urban employment | 256.4 | 264.8 | 273.3 | 283.1 | 293.5 | 302.1 |
| *Including:* | | | | | | |
| State-owned enterprises | 68.8 | 67.1 | 64.9 | 64.3 | 64.2 | 64.5 |
| Collective units | 10.0 | 9.0 | 8.1 | 7.6 | 7.2 | 6.6 |
| Private | 46.2 | 52.9 | 61.4 | 68.4 | 76.6 | 83.7 |
| Foreign-invested enterprises | 8.6 | 10.3 | 12.5 | 14.1 | 15.8 | 16.2 |
| Self-employed | 23.8 | 25.2 | 27.8 | 30.1 | 33.1 | 36.1 |
| Rural employment | 487.9 | 487.2 | 484.9 | 480.9 | 476.4 | 472.7 |
| *Including:* | | | | | | |
| Town & village enterprises | 135.7 | 138.7 | 142.7 | 146.8 | 150.9 | 154.5 |
| Private | 17.5 | 20.2 | 23.7 | 26.3 | 26.7 | – |
| Self-employed | 22.6 | 20.7 | 21.2 | 21.5 | 21.9 | – |
| Total employment | 744.3 | 752.0 | 758.3 | 764.0 | 769.9 | 774.8 |

Source: *China Statistical Yearbook*, China Statistical Abstract 2009

youth trends in China, describes this as the birth of individualism. Eager to express themselves in a way their parents never did (or could), young Chinese consumers accessorise their mobile phones, create elaborate online alter-egos and assimilate fashions from around the world into their own personal style. To do this, they use both foreign and local brands.

Chinese consumers may be loyal to the motherland, but they still aspire to foreign brands. Why? Because foreign brands traditionally stand for quality, status and reliability. Back in 1998, the top three brands in China were foreign: Motorola, Nokia and Ericsson. Motorola's fully owned Tianjin subsidiary – one of only a handful such fully owned enterprises in China at the time – accounted for 50% of all mobile phone sales and an astonishing 70% of pager sales.

How times have changed. The domestic competition has learnt quickly and now dominates the mobile phone sector. Nowadays Chinese consumers seek foreign brands with cachet, though still valuing quality and reliability: BMW, Rolex, Sony and L'Oréal are particular favourites. The success of L'Oréal, for example, stems from the company's ability "to bring the best new products to market using the latest technologies for both women and men", according to one British executive. It understands the market needs and has a passion for what it does. In 2008, L'Oréal started using the Asian expertise of its Japanese subsidiaries, Nihon L'Oréal and Shu Uemura Cosmetics, to localise its product range more effectively for Chinese consumers. Other companies also localise their product offerings, particularly those in fast-food businesses. For example, KFC sells *youtiao*, a typically Shanghainese breakfast dish made from deep-fried twisted dough, Beijing Duck-style chicken rolls, Cantonese-style pumpkin *congee*, and *gongbao jiding*, a spicy Sichuanese chicken dish.

Yet when it comes to day-to-day products Chinese consumers still seek reassurance from the size and scale of the companies that manufacture the products they buy, believing that the bigger a company is, the more likely its products are to be well-made and reliable. Coca-Cola, KFC, Unilever and Procter & Gamble trade on their size rather than their foreign origins. However, this approach has its risks, since such companies also become targets for opportunists seeking to exploit their market profile for personal gain. Jean-Michel Dumont, chairman of Ruder Finn Asia, says:

> *Big multinational companies are often attacked by consumers looking for financial or other compensation, or even by media groups seeking to create controversy – and so boost advertising income. Both often ride on a "local-David versus foreign Goliath" wave, making such attacks all the more credible.*

Although Chinese consumers are brand aware, they are also fickle, says Tom Doctoroff, north-east Asia director and Greater China CEO of JWT, a global advertising agency. Most consumers have little or no brand heritage, but instead have been bombarded with hundreds of new brands entering the market over the space of a few short years. This can make advertising difficult and expensive. Marketers are advised to develop and maintain consistent, straightforward messages that communicate effectively to the right consumer segment. They should also avoid potentially sensitive topics. An advertising campaign released by US sports brand Nike in 2004 featured LeBron James, an American basketball star, fighting and defeating a computer-generated Kung Fu master, much to the indignation of Chinese consumers, who complained so vociferously that the government banned the advertisement later that year.

### ... and technology ...

Chinese consumers have embraced technology with perhaps even more enthusiasm than consumers elsewhere in the world, largely because it opens a door to communication and the outside world that was closed to previous generations.

Is there still a role for television in advertising or is it all going online? In 2009 Barry Colman, group account director at McCann-Erickson, put this question to 50 university students from four cities. They answered that they watched (and would continue to watch) television and read magazines to get information about products, but that they went online for something different: to bring it all to life. Colman believes that effective marketing requires a mixture of television commercials and online advertising, with online advertising taking the messaging further.

### ... and even luxury

Major luxury brands have a short history in China, with only a handful dating back to the early 1990s. Ermenegildo Zegna sneaked into China in 1991, with Louis Vuitton and Montblanc following in 1992 and Bally, Dunhill, Ferragamo, Givenchy, Rolex and Versace in 1993. These brands mainly ran concessions or small stores-within-stores in the few high-quality department stores that existed at the time in the big three cities of Beijing, Shanghai and Guangzhou. These early entrants were followed by Hugo Boss in 1994, Prada in 1995 and Burberry in 1996. In 1997, Gucci and Hermès set up partnerships with local agents to sell their products in local department stores. Further liberalisation of the retail sector attracted more luxury brands in the early 2000s, though a dearth of quality retail space initially hampered brand expansion.

The subsequent emergence of luxury shopping malls and rapid growth of an aspirational middle class has made China the world's second largest market for luxury goods, reaching $8.6 billion or 25% of the world total, according to the World Luxury Association. Goldman Sachs, a US investment bank, predicts that China will overtake Japan to become the world's largest market for luxury goods with 29% of the global market in 2015. Already more than 300,000 Chinese have a net worth of more than $1m; a study by consulting firm McKinsey & Co. forecasts that this number will rise to an estimated 4.4m by 2015, giving China the world's fourth largest population of wealthy households.

Paul Husband, founder of Husband Retail Consulting, a luxury retail planning consultancy based in Hong Kong, has watched the luxury retail market grow in fits and starts on the mainland since he founded his company in 1998. Yet many brands have gone in big, only to be humbled. Husband stresses that the location, management quality and above all an appropriate "retail mix" (ensuring that your luxury apparel store is not sandwiched between a local burger bar and a pharmacy, for example) are crucial to luxury brands succeeding with Chinese consumers.

In advertising, the biggest spenders have traditionally been local brands, though in recent years multinational consumer goods firms have entered the top ten. Global personal care and fast-food brands are edging out their local counterparts, and this is likely to continue as Chinese consumers' spending power grows.

Table 3.3 **Top ten advertisers by adspend, 2008**

| Rank | Company | Expenditure (Rmb bn) | Rank | Company | Expenditure (Rmb bn) |
|---|---|---|---|---|---|
| 1 | Procter & Gamble | 29.1 | 6 | China Mobile Telecom | 5.0 |
| 2 | Harbin Pharmaceutical Group | 17.4 | 7 | Coca-Cola | 4.8 |
| 3 | Unilever | 13.2 | 8 | Hangzhou Wahaha Group | 4.0 |
| 4 | L'Oréal (China) | 9.0 | 9 | Colgate Palmolive | 4.0 |
| 5 | Yum! Brands | 7.9 | 10 | Nice Group | 3.8 |

Source: Nielsen Media Research

## Where to invest

The sheer scale of China and the cultural variety within its borders are astounding. Covering 9.56m sq. km (around 20,000 sq. km bigger than the United States), most of the country's 1.33 billion people live in the centre and east of the country and this is where the largest cities are. China has 651 cities of which some 113 have a population of over 1m. The largest include Shanghai (15.6m), Beijing (13.1m), Guangzhou (11m), Shenzhen (8.5m), Tianjin (5.2m) and Chongqing (5.1m).

Most multinational companies and brands focus on the first-tier cities. But with competition intensifying and consumer segments growing in inland or smaller urban markets, many have started to look further afield. Some, such as US companies Wrigley, Coca-Cola and Procter & Gamble, have been selling into second- and third-tier cities, as well as rural areas, since the 1990s. Also in these markets have been East Asian companies, particularly President, a Taiwanese maker of instant noodles and snack foods.

Table 3.4 **China's 20 largest cities, 2009**

| City | Metropolitan area population (m) | Administrative level |
| --- | --- | --- |
| Shanghai | 17.0 | Municipality |
| Beijing | 13.2 | Municipality |
| Guangzhou | 12.0 | Provincial capital |
| Shenzhen | 8.6 | Special economic zone city |
| Tianjin | 8.2 | Municipality |
| Chongqing | 7.5 | Municipality |
| Hong Kong | 7.1 | Special administrative region |
| Dongguan | 6.9 | Prefecture |
| Nanjing | 6.8 | Provincial capital |
| Wuhan | 6.6 | Provincial capital |
| Hangzhou | 6.3 | Provincial capital |
| Shenyang | 5.1 | Provincial capital |
| Harbin | 4.8 | Provincial capital |
| Chengdu | 4.8 | Provincial capital |
| Hefei | 4.7 | Provincial capital |
| Zhengzhou | 4.4 | Provincial capital |
| Jinan | 4.0 | Provincial capital |
| Qingdao | 3.8 | Sub-provincial city |
| Xi'an | 3.8 | Provincial capital |
| Nanchang | 3.8 | Provincial capital |

Source: National Bureau of Statistics

Despite China's vast size, foreign investment has focused, for good reasons, on three main regions:

- Guangdong's Pearl River Delta (PRD), with its proximity to Hong Kong and international trade;
- Shanghai and the Yangtze River Delta (YRD), with its capitalist roots and port access both inland and overseas;
- Beijing, as the seat of power for the highly centralised national government.

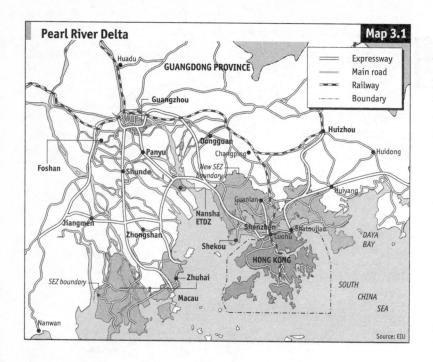

**Pearl River Delta**     Map 3.1

Source: EIU

### Pearl River Delta

As tens of thousands of companies have sought new light-industrial bases across Guangdong, so investment and wealth have expanded from Guangzhou and Shenzhen into the smaller cities of Dongguan, Foshan, Huizhou, Zhongshan and Zhuhai. This region was the first engine of Chinese growth in the 1980s, with Hong Kong and Taiwanese companies setting up operations, but it has become a victim of its own success. Higher wages and improved living conditions have raised operating costs to the point where investors are looking elsewhere for low-cost manufacturing. The PRD is still the primary manufacturing centre for consumer electronics, but it is focusing on innovation and value-added manufacturing in a bid to regain its competitiveness. It can also rely on its excellent port infrastructure to serve export companies, both foreign and local.

### Yangtze River Delta

Shanghai's re-emergence as the country's commercial and financial centre has taken less than 20 years.[1] Just as the PRD owned the 1980s, so Shanghai and the YRD owned the 1990s, thanks to massive and unswerving central

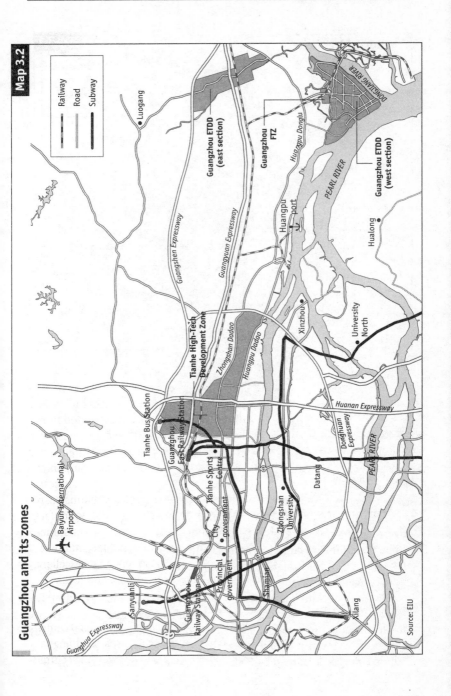

**Map 3.2**

**Guangzhou and its zones**

Source: EIU

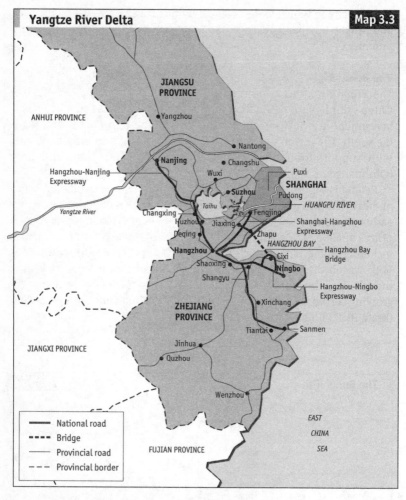

**Yangtze River Delta** — Map 3.3

government support; a geographically strategic position on the coast where the country's largest river meets the sea; and a developing market of some 300m consumers increasingly connected by one of the best transport networks in the country.

Shanghai's wealth has emanated outwards to smaller cities within the YRD, building numerous clusters of manufacturing, R&D and services. This has resulted in one of the greatest concentrations of wealth in the country, as well as some of the best cities in which to do business. These include Hangzhou (named by Forbes, a US business magazine, as the best

Chinese city in which to do business for five consecutive years, 2004–08) and Ningbo (Zhejiang province), and Kunshan, Suzhou and Wuxi (Jiangsu province).

### The Bohai Rim

The Bohai Rim, including the Beijing-Tianjin Corridor, has emerged as China's third major destination for foreign investment, adding a northern investment hub to complement the YRD in the centre and the PRD in the south. The region's growth has been dependent primarily on Beijing, with support from other major cities (Tianjin, Qingdao) and ports (Qinhuangdao, Yantai).

Beijing is typical of many northern cities in being a traditional centre of heavy industry in contrast to Shanghai and Guangdong. Since the early 1980s, Beijing has been the location for some 10,000 representative offices opened by foreign companies. A host of multinational companies, including global players such as General Electric, Hewlett-Packard, Ford, Volkswagen and Motorola, have their China headquarters in Beijing, though the attraction of Shanghai as an investor-friendly centre of the growing consumer market of the Yangtze River Delta has prompted some (Kraft, BHP Billiton) to move there.

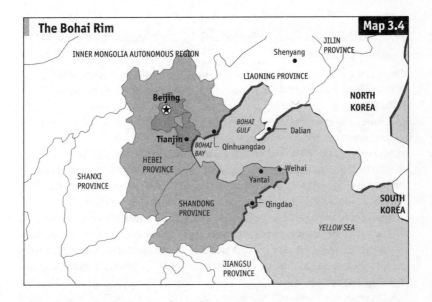

Map 3.4 The Bohai Rim

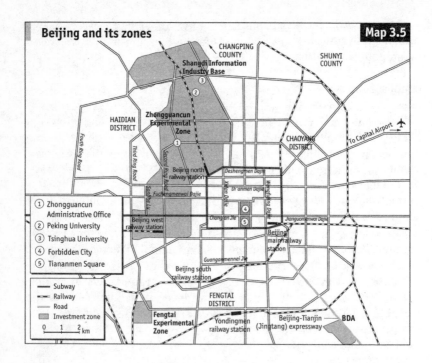

Map 3.5 — Beijing and its zones

### A zone of its own

Why bother going into an economic zone when you can build your own? Finnish telecoms company Nokia did not go quite that far, but it did carve out a part of the Beijing Economic-Technological Development Area (BDA) for its own use and call it the Xingwang Industrial Park. Established in 2000, the park was a partnership between Nokia and two powerful local partners – the Beijing municipality government and the BDA – and has subsequently received some $1.2 billion in investment. In 2008, Nokia set up a new R&D centre with some 2,000 researchers; the same year, its total China revenues from domestic sales and exports exceeded $13 billion. Given Nokia's pulling power, a number of suppliers, such as US integrated-circuit-maker RF Micro Devices, have found it expedient to move into the park. A senior manager at one such supplier believes Nokia has got it right in creating its own manufacturing cluster, but that life has been easier for the firm over the past ten years because of its state partners – and the support it enjoyed from central government.

Overshadowed by the national capital, Tianjin municipality is roughly 100km south-east on the coast. Yet the city has a world-class port, an urban population of nearly 12m and some of the top investment zones in the country. Tianjin Economic and Technological Development Area, established in 1984 with a state-approved area of 33 sq. km, consistently rates among the best of China's special investment locations.

## Beyond the big three regions

The big three regions offer proximity to major ports and consumer segments, but these markets can become saturated and overcrowded. Other large-scale coastal cities – Dalian, Shenyang and Qingdao in the north, Xiamen (home to US computer firm Dell) and Fuzhou in the south-east, and Wuhan, Chongqing and Chengdu in the interior – offer large markets and efficient infrastructure. Clusters have developed based on industries or country of origin (South Korean companies favour the Shandong coastline around Qingdao, where a large Korean community is based), often because of historical connections (Japan has a strong colonial legacy in the port city of Dalian) or because companies' local partners are based there. In the car industry, for example, foreign companies are expected to set up manufacturing facilities where their local partners already have plants as part of their technology transfer and labour arrangements.

### Second- and third-tier markets

Multinational companies are not limited to first-tier cities. China has roughly 100 more cities with populations of more than 1m, many of them offering fresh markets for foreign companies. Some, such as fast-food giants KFC and McDonald's, Taiwanese instant-noodle-maker President and Hong Kong retailers Giordano and Bossini, have been pushing into second- and third-tier markets for many years. Now IT multinational companies, such as Dell, Hewlett-Packard and Nokia, are moving into these markets as their distribution channels develop and their cheaper products become more affordable for consumers in these markets. Rural retail sales have responded since 2009 with a new confidence that raises hopes for increased domestic demand.

Lower-profile cities offer attractive conditions for manufacturers too. Anglo-Dutch consumer goods firm Unilever has based its household and personal care production in Hefei, the capital of Anhui province, where it has the largest production site by volume of any Unilever site in the world. Meanwhile, since 2005 Intel has invested more than $400m in

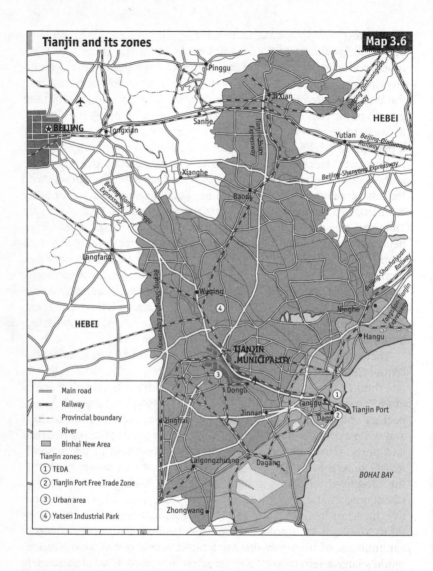

**Tianjin and its zones**

Map 3.6

Zhuanghua

Pinggu

Jixian

HEBEI

BEIJING

Tongxian

Sanhe

Yutian · *Beijing-Qinhuangdao Railway*

*Tianjin-Jixian Expressway*

*Beijing-Shenyang Expressway*

*Datong-Qinhuangdao Railway*

Xianghe

Baodi

*Beijing Tianjin-Tanggu Expressway*

Langfang

*Beijing-Shanghai Expressway*

Wuqing

④

HEBEI

Ninghe

*Beijing-Shanhaiguan Railway*

*Tangshan-Tianjin Expressway*

Hangu

TIANJIN MUNICIPALITY

③

Dongli

Tanggu

①

Jinnan

Dagu

②

Tianjin Port

Jinghai

Caigongzhuang

Dagang

BOHAI BAY

Zhongwang

Legend:
- — Main road
- —■— Railway
- ----- Provincial boundary
- — River
- ▓ Binhai New Area

Tianjin zones:
- ① TEDA
- ② Tianjin Port Free Trade Zone
- ③ Urban area
- ④ Yatsen Industrial Park

testing and assembly facility in Chengdu (the US chipmaker has had a testing and assembly plant in Shanghai's Waigaoqiao Free Trade Zone since 1998 and in 2007 set up a $2.5 billion plant in Dalian), benefiting from an educated and well-trained workforce – and doubtless winning brownie points with the central government for supporting Beijing's "Develop the West" investment campaign.

*Going west*

The rapid growth of China's coastal provinces in the 1990s, as a result of export-fuelled investment, improved living conditions and created a growing gap between China's eastern and western regions. A "Develop the West" policy was set in motion in 2000 in response to the startling growth of the coastal regions. China's own definition of what constitutes its western regions essentially covers "more remote and frontier areas, a perception which often gives rise to an assumption that the western regions are 'backward'", according to Doris Ma and Tim Summers, authors of a Chatham House paper on inland growth.[2] The policy covers six inland provinces (Gansu, Guizhou, Qinghai, Shaanxi, Sichuan and Yunnan), five autonomous regions (Guangxi, Inner Mongolia, Ningxia, Tibet and Xinjiang) and Chongqing, the fourth municipality (the others being Beijing, Shanghai and Tianjin). This region contains more than two-thirds of the country's geographical area but less than one-third of its population – and less than one-fifth of its economic output. However, based on data that show a substantial increase in overall GDP across the western regions, Ma and Summers believe that the western regions – with continuing fixed-asset investment – will become an increasingly important part of China's economic development.

There are a number of benefits for foreign investors in western and central China, including cheap land and labour (wages can be as little as one-third of those in coastal provinces) and various government incentives. The response from multinational investors has been sluggish, largely because of infrastructure weaknesses, underdeveloped consumer markets and the massive distances required to transport goods to coastal markets and ports. Yet the government's relentless investment in the region is slowly drawing in more foreign investment, and for some companies the incentives will make comparatively well-developed cities such as Chongqing and Chengdu, Sichuan's provincial capital, increasingly attractive. Investors in Chengdu include Microsoft, which runs an R&D centre for its Xbox games console, and Cochlear, an Australian manufacturer of ear implants, which set up a research project in the city in 2009. Intel, the world's largest semiconductor-maker, first moved to Sichuan in 2003. In 2009 it announced plans to increase investment in its chip-testing and packaging plant in Chengdu from $375m to $600m.

## Investment zones: still worth it?

Investment zones are by no means unique to China. Emerging markets around the world have used carefully controlled areas – often starting as

Table 3.5 **Urban living expenditure by region, 2008**

|  | Expenditure per head (Rmb) | Annual change (%) |
|---|---|---|
| National average | 11,243 | 29.3 |
| *South/south-western region* | | |
| Guangdong | 15,528 | 24.9 |
| Fujian | 12,501 | 27.5 |
| Hainan | 9,408 | 32.0 |
| *Eastern region* | | |
| Shanghai | 19,398 | 31.4 |
| Zhejiang | 15,158 | 13.6 |
| Jiangsu | 11,978 | 24.4 |
| *North/north-eastern region* | | |
| Beijing | 16,460 | 11.0 |
| Tianjin | 13,422 | 27.2 |
| Liaoning | 11,231 | 40.6 |
| Shandong | 11,007 | 30.0 |
| Jilin | 9,729 | 32.3 |
| Hebei | 9,087 | 23.7 |
| Heilongjiang | 8,623 | 29.6 |
| *Western region* | | |
| Chongqing | 11,147 | 18.6 |
| Inner Mongolia | 10,829 | 41.2 |
| Shaanxi | 9,772 | 29.4 |
| Sichuan | 9,679 | 28.6 |
| Guangxi | 9,627 | 41.7 |
| Ningxia | 9,558 | 32.6 |
| Yunnan | 9,077 | 23.0 |
| Xinjiang | 8,669 | 28.8 |
| Guizhou | 8,349 | 21.9 |
| Tibet | 8,323 | 34.4 |
| Gansu | 8,309 | 19.1 |
| Qinghai | 8,193 | 25.5 |

|  | Expenditure per head (Rmb) | Annual change (%) |
| --- | --- | --- |
| Central region | | |
| Hunan | 9,945 | 21.7 |
| Anhui | 9,524 | 30.6 |
| Hubei | 9,477 | 28.1 |
| Henan | 8,837 | 32.2 |
| Shanxi | 8,807 | 22.8 |
| Jiangxi | 8,717 | 31.2 |

Source: China Statistical Abstract 2009

trial operations – in which to test the effect of new foreign-investment policies without jeopardising the wider economy. However, in the space of less than three decades investment zones have played a crucial role in propelling China's economy from nowhere to one of the top three economies in the world. Yet has China's accession to the World Trade Organisation rendered these zones redundant?

Modern China's foray into investment zones began in 1980 as the open-door policy sought to attract much-needed foreign investment to kick-start the economy. The creation of the fab four "special economic zones" (SEZs) in Shenzhen, Zhuhai, Shantou and Xiamen was followed by the establishment of 14 "economic and technological development zones" (ETDZs) in 1984, along with a fifth SEZ, Hainan, in 1988. The zones quickly began to demonstrate their value as Hong Kong, Taiwanese and domestic entrepreneurs capitalised on low land and labour costs combined with attractive investment incentives. Fast-forward 20 years and by 2007 China had a total of 1,568 zones, comprising some 222 national-level zones and 1,346 provincial and local-level zones – too many for the central government, which subsequently forced the consolidation or closure of most regional zones and encouraged foreign investors to focus on the 200 or so national-level zones.

Elizabeth Cheng, editor of the Economist Intelligence Unit's *China Hand*, sees merit in the zones. The centrally approved investment zones are generally well laid out with basic amenities in plentiful supply, away from densely crowded, rundown urban cores. A number of such zones are becoming new city centres; the Suzhou Industrial Park, for example, will house the city government offices as old Suzhou is being preserved with its historical artefacts. So although the zones will not be as special

Table 3.6 **Disposable income per head by city, 2008**

| City | Per head (Rmb) |
| --- | --- |
| Dongguan (Guangdong) | 30,275 |
| Shenzhen (Guangdong) | 26,729 |
| Shanghai | 26,675 |
| Wenzhou (Zhejiang) | 26,172 |
| Guangzhou (Guangdong) | 25,317 |
| Ningbo (Zhejiang) | 25,304 |
| Beijing | 24,725 |
| Hangzhou (Zhejiang) | 24,104 |
| Xiamen (Fujian) | 23,948 |
| Suzhou (Jiangsu) | 23,867 |
| Wuxi (Jiangsu) | 23,605 |
| Nanjing (Jiangsu) | 23,123 |
| Foshan (Guangdong) | 22,494 |
| Changzhou (Jiangsu) | 21,592 |
| Jinhua (Zhejiang) | 21,408 |
| Zhuhai (Guangdong) | 20,949 |
| Jinan (Shandong) | 20,802 |
| Qingdao (Shandong) | 20,464 |
| Quanzhou (Fujian) | 20,420 |
| Hohhot (Inner Mongolia) | 20,267 |
| Tianjin | 19,423 |
| Yantai (Shandong) | 19,350 |
| Fuzhou (Fujian) | 19,009 |
| Nantong (Jiangsu) | 18,903 |
| Changsha (Hunan) | 18,282 |
| National | 15,781 |

Source: The Collection of Statistics on China Economy & Social Development, 2008–09

Table 3.7 **Utilised foreign direct investment in central and western China, $m**

|  | 2008 | 2007 | 2006 | 2005 | 2004 |
|---|---|---|---|---|---|
| Chongqing | 2,729 | 1,085 | 696 | 516 | 252 |
| Sichuan | 3,340[a] | 2,011[a] | 1,470[a] | 1,100[a] | 365 |
| Guizhou | 149 | 127 | 94 | 108 | 63 |
| Yunnan | – | 395 | 302 | 189[a] | 142 |
| Shaanxi | 1,370[a] | 1,195[a] | 925[a] | 628[a] | 141 |
| Gansu | 128 | 118 | 30 | 20 | 35 |
| Qinghai | 220 | 310 | 275 | 266 | 353 |
| Ningxia | 121[a] | 170[a] | 138[a] | 141[a] | 67 |
| Xinjiang | 190 | 125 | 104 | 47 | 40 |
| Inner Mongolia | 2,651 | 2,149 | 1,741 | 1,186 | 343 |
| Guangxi | 971 | 684 | 447 | 379 | 296 |

Note: utilised FDI is investment that has been made, as opposed to "contractual" FDI that has been pledged but not yet spent.
a Includes foreign loans.
Sources: Local government estimates; CEIC

as they were with tax incentives, they will have a head start in lifestyle and modern conveniences.

John Williams of International SOS believes in the long-term future of investment zones, especially SEZs, because there is a much stronger "can do" approach from the zone authorities which "creates a stronger foundation for partnership and success". Significantly, says Williams:

> Chinese officials are now appraised against KPIs and they
> work much in the same way now as do managers of foreign
> companies.

The vast majority of China's investment zones must ultimately close, having served their purpose of helping with national economic development. Yet some will remain as testbeds of further economic reform, particularly in areas such as technological innovation and in (mainly inland) regions that have yet to benefit fully from the market economy. For the time being, investment zones remain an option for foreign investors.

China's five special economic zones — Map 3.7

*Special economic zones*

China's first foray into investment zones came in 1984 with the creation by Deng Xiaoping of four SEZs in the southern provinces of Guangdong and Fujian: Shenzhen, Shantou, Xiamen and Zhuhai. In 1988, one more was added in the form of Hainan (an island south of the mainland and part of Guangdong province until it became a province in 1988).

*Economic and technological development zones*

China's first ETDZs were originally established in 1988 in 14 designated cities as an incentive for foreign investors to bring more technology into China. By 2008, there were 54 ETDZs offering various incentives to foreign companies, though in line with China's tax equalisation policy (see Chapter 5) the 15% income tax rates previously offered in these areas were scheduled to rise gradually to 25% in 2012, according to the State Council.

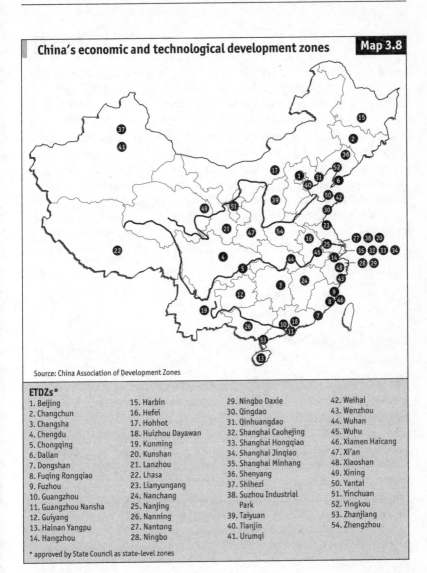

## China's economic and technological development zones

**Map 3.8**

Source: China Association of Development Zones

**ETDZs***

1. Beijing
2. Changchun
3. Changsha
4. Chengdu
5. Chongqing
6. Dalian
7. Dongshan
8. Fuqing Rongqiao
9. Fuzhou
10. Guangzhou
11. Guangzhou Nansha
12. Guiyang
13. Hainan Yangpu
14. Hangzhou
15. Harbin
16. Hefei
17. Hohhot
18. Huizhou Dayawan
19. Kunming
20. Kunshan
21. Lanzhou
22. Lhasa
23. Lianyungang
24. Nanchang
25. Nanjing
26. Nanning
27. Nantong
28. Ningbo
29. Ningbo Daxie
30. Qingdao
31. Qinhuangdao
32. Shanghai Caohejing
33. Shanghai Hongqiao
34. Shanghai Jinqiao
35. Shanghai Minhang
36. Shenyang
37. Shihezi
38. Suzhou Industrial Park
39. Taiyuan
40. Tianjin
41. Urumqi
42. Weihai
43. Wenzhou
44. Wuhan
45. Wuhu
46. Xiamen Haicang
47. Xi'an
48. Xiaoshan
49. Xining
50. Yantai
51. Yinchuan
52. Yingkou
53. Zhanjiang
54. Zhengzhou

* approved by State Council as state-level zones

## Foreign trade zones

As the SEZs enjoyed growing success in providing a controlled environment in which to encourage the manufacture of export-destined products by foreign companies enjoying preferential investor treatment, there emerged a need for a more effective import and export infrastructure to bring in raw materials and take out finished products. The foreign trade zones (FTZs, also known as bonded zones) met that need, offering duty-free import and storage of machinery, equipment, raw materials, goods and products, availability of office space and good infrastructure – including reasonably efficient customs clearance. A total of 15 ports were allocated FTZ status, becoming free-trade and export-processing centres for multinational companies all down the east coast, and in a few cases in border areas (see Table 3.8). Korgas Port (Xinjiang region) became the 16th FTZ in 2009 as part of a trading initiative between China and neighbouring Kazakhstan.

Table 3.8 **China's free-trade zones**

| | |
| --- | --- |
| Dalian | Liaoning province |
| Fuzhou | Fujian province |
| Guangzhou | Guangdong province |
| Haikou | Hainan province |
| Ningbo | Zhejiang province |
| Qingdao | Shandong province |
| Shanghai Waigaoqiao | Shanghai municipality |
| Shantou | Guangdong province |
| Shenzhen Futian | Guangdong province |
| Shenzhen Shatoujiao | Guangdong province |
| Shenzhen Yantian | Guangdong province |
| Tianjin Port | Tianjin province |
| Xiamen Xiangyu | Fujian province |
| Zhangjiagang | Jiangsu province |
| Zhuhai | Guangdong province |

Source: China Association of Development Zones

## Export-processing zones

In 2000, China also began operating export-processing zones (EPZs) within the ETDZs. There are now 25 EPZs, not all of them on the coast. Overall they have been extremely successful, their principal advantage over FTZs being that companies operating in an EPZ pay no value-added tax (VAT) because the goods are defined as exports. This also enables companies selling to EPZ businesses to claim export refunds. The only regulatory constraint is that companies in the EPZs must restrict their operations exclusively to export processing.

Table 3.9 **China's export-processing and development zones**

| | | |
|---|---|---|
| Beihai | Kunming | Shenyang (Zhangshi) |
| Beijing Tianzhu | Kunshan | Shenzhen |
| Changshu | Langfang | Suzhou Industrial Park |
| Changzhou | Lianyungang | Suzhou National New & High-tech Industrial Development Zone |
| Chengdu | Mianyang | Tianjin |
| Chenzhou | Nanjing | Urumqi |
| Chongqing | Nansha | Weifang |
| Cixi | Nantong | Weihai |
| Dalian | Ningbo | Wuhan |
| Fuqing | Qingdao | Wuhu |
| Fuzhou | Qinhuangdao | Wujiang |
| Guangzhou | Quanzhou | Wuxi |
| Hangzhou | Shanghai Caohejing | Wuzhong |
| Hohhot | Shanghai Jiading | Xiamen |
| Huizhou | Shanghai Jinqiao | Xi'an |
| Hunchun | Shanghai Minhang | Yangzhou |
| Jiaxing | Shanghai Qingpu | Yantai |
| Jinan | Shanghai Songjiang | Zhengzhou |
| Jiujiang | Shenyang | Zhenjiang |

Source: China Association of Development Zones

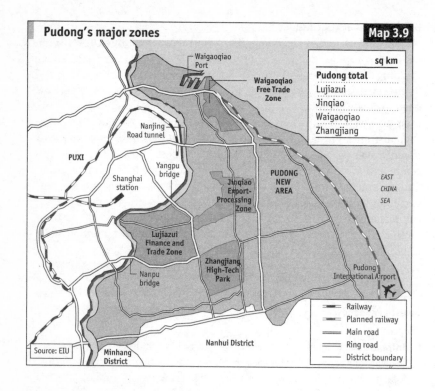

Map 3.9

**Pudong's major zones**

| | sq km |
|---|---|
| **Pudong total** | |
| Lujiazui | |
| Jinqiao | |
| Waigaoqiao | |
| Zhangjiang | |

Waigaoqiao Port
Waigaoqiao Free Trade Zone
Nanjing Road tunnel
PUXI
Yangpu bridge
Shanghai station
Jinqiao Export-Processing Zone
PUDONG NEW AREA
EAST CHINA SEA
Lujiazui Finance and Trade Zone
Zhangjiang High-Tech Park
Nanpu bridge
Pudong International Airport
Nanhui District
Source: EIU
Minhang District

Railway
Planned railway
Main road
Ring road
District boundary

## High technology development zones

As part of its long-term policy to move its economy up the value chain the Chinese government allowed some cities to designate high technology development zones (HTDZs) in a bid to attract foreign high-tech companies. Of the 53 national-level HTDZs set up, most are located in university districts, which typically lack space for development and have poor infrastructure. Having failed to attract true high-tech investors, local officials with responsibility for these zones have been forced to accept lower-tech businesses seeking to win high-tech status and the benefits that go with it.

## Border zones

China runs 14 border zones, most of them approved by the State Council in 1992. They are fairly evenly scattered along the borders of Guangxi, Yunnan, Xinjiang, Inner Mongolia and Heilongjiang, and are intended to promote economic co-operation with neighbouring countries. Yunnan's border zones at Ruili and Wanding, for instance, promote cross-border trade with Myanmar, and its Hekou border zone to the east trades with Vietnam.

## Pudong: the odd one out

Some zones are unique. Pudong New Area was born in 1990 out of a need to create a financial centre for China. Shanghai, frozen out for more than 40 years by a suspicious CPC leadership that viewed this once-capitalist enclave with apprehension, was released back into the wild to rediscover its capitalist roots. Deluged with fixed investment from the centre and given national-level authority to approve foreign investment, Pudong emerged from a misty, featureless estuary studded with the odd decrepit go-down to become a high-rise jungle that quickly dwarfed the colonial architecture of the Bund across the river. Solid support from then President Jiang Zemin and "economic czar" Vice-premier Zhu Rongji, both of whom had spent time in Shanghai, ensured the city's stellar growth.

### Investment zones

#### The pros

- ■ **Infrastructure.** Centrally approved zones have modern infrastructure (including housing for workers, a significant bonus for employees) and remain a priority for local government when it comes to power, utilities and communications.
- ■ **Location.** The majority of investment zones are located in coastal areas. Access to ports and airports is a major factor in foreign companies' decisions to invest. Hong Kong companies, for example, chose neighbouring Shenzhen because products could easily be assembled and exported.
- ■ **Test labs.** The government will retain some zones – and create new ones – to serve as laboratories for economic or technological reform. It set up experimental zones in Sichuan and Chongqing in 2007, and the same year announced the creation of two new "environmental zones" around Wuhan (Hubei province) and Changsha (Hunan province).
- ■ **Flexibility.** Zone authorities are generally more open-minded and flexible towards foreign investor needs than other government officials. Management at outstanding zones such as the Tianjin Economic Development Area (TEDA) typically feature young and progressive officials.
- ■ **Status.** Major centrally approved zones often enjoy central or local government support and may serve as hubs for local development plans, thereby conferring status on companies within the zone.
- ■ **Clusters.** "United we stand, divided we fall": foreign investors operating in a

manufacturing cluster within a zone gain a group advantage when negotiating deals with the local administration. Clusters also help attract skilled labour and pool knowledge and experiences.

*The cons*
- ▨ **Rising land costs.** Strengths can also be weaknesses. The strategic position of many investment zones in coastal areas near ports and airports initially attracted foreign investment and so helped with local economic development. However, the long-term result – rising land costs – is eroding their cost-effectiveness.
- ▨ **Few local partners present.** In the old days when partnerships were heavily restricted, setting up in an investment zone with other foreign companies made sense. As investment restrictions have eased, foreign companies, which are now allowed take increasingly large stakes in local companies, are choosing to leave the relative security of the zones and step into the outside world.
- ▨ **Inland zones still lag behind.** Despite consistent state support, many zones in central and western regions continue to face basic infrastructure challenges and have less experience of dealing with foreign investors, which sometimes manifests itself in the form of inflexibility towards investor needs.
- ▨ **Tax incentives (some zones till 2012).** The Enterprise Income Tax law in 2008 removed the chief attraction for foreign-invested enterprises: preferential tax treatment in the form of tax holidays, lower rates or deferred payments. Foreign companies that have high-tech status or are willing to invest in central and western regions may qualify for lower tax rates.

## Infrastructure

Building an efficient infrastructure for a country the size of China is an immensely complex task requiring massive, unstinting state investment. The government has succeeded in creating power, communications and transport networks for most coastal provinces and major cities, but substantial parts of the country lack adequate coverage. The global recession has exacerbated a power glut resulting from the creation of new capacity in response to repeated brown-outs caused by surging electricity demand in the booming coastal provinces in 2005–06. Coal-fired thermal power accounts for some 80% of China's electricity generation, with new coal-fired thermal power stations opening at a rate of roughly one every three days. China needs to power economic development in coastal provinces, even though this puts even greater pressure on China's creaking rail network to transport ever more coal to the coast from the north and west. Coal freight accounts for 40% of freight and passenger transport on China's rail network.

Other infrastructure is also catching up. Fixed-line telephone networks cover 80% of the population, but large areas of western China have little or no coverage. China's mobile phone population exceeded 700m in 2009, though reception was far superior in coastal provinces than in the central and western regions of the country.

Meanwhile, the national road network has grown rapidly, but at the expense of the rail system, which was neglected for many years. Massive state funding for nationally approved investment zones such as the SEZs and Pudong New Area have sucked in much of the capital (and FDI) that could have gone elsewhere.

### Keep on trucking

China continues to develop its transport network in a bid to reach all points of its vast geography. Massive investment has helped, particularly in the road and air sectors. In 1996, China had 3,400 km of expressways; by 2007 this had grown to 53,900 km, linking every province and county (though still far behind the US with 93,000 km); airports and aircraft across the country have been upgraded. There was less investment in rail and water transport in the 1990s, though this was redressed in the 2000s. The Three Gorges Dam helped make the Yangtze River up to Chongqing navigable all year round.[3]

Shanghai's pre-Expo boom in transport infrastructure also underlined the scale and speed of progress. In 2008–09, the city embarked on a project to build nine subway lines simultaneously, with more than 100 stations. Other projects included the Bund Passage, a two-level road tunnel stretching more than 3km from Yan'an East Road northwards under Suzhou Creek to Hongkou district. For this project, China used indigenous technologies developed to deal with Shanghai's marshy foundations. (Soviet experts consulted about building a metro system in the city in 1956 concluded that the task would be like "digging holes in bean curd".)

Around two-thirds of companies now use road haulage as their primary mode of transport, largely because of the growing road network and the problems associated with rail. The Ministry of Transport's long-term "7-9-18" scheme – involving seven expressways fanning out from Beijing in a hub-and-spoke pattern, nine expressways running north-south down the country and 18 routes running east-west – began in 2005 and by 2010 was already half-completed. Upon its completion, most of China's population should be able to reach an expressway in less than an hour. China has some 3.5m km of rural highways.

Road cargo is limited to inter-provincial or at best regional operations, thanks to a still-developing road network and local protectionism restricting inter-provincial and inter-city operations. Multinational companies are obliged to partner with more than one trucking company (and often over a dozen) to gain adequate reach into their markets. China's estimated 1m trucking companies range from major regional and provincial players with fleets of thousands of vehicles to city-wide businesses and far smaller one-man-and-a-truck operations. Generally, size matters with trucking companies, though a careful assessment of fleet quality is also essential. Chinese trucks are often poorly maintained and of poor quality, particularly away from the coastal provinces where old local vehicles are more common than Japanese and European brands. Less than 20% of trucks are containerised, and specialised refrigerated and air-conditioned vehicles for perishable goods are a rarity. Long-haul road freight is increasing nevertheless, and hundreds of long-distance trucking companies now operate along major expressways between top-tier cities – particularly Beijing, Shanghai and Guangzhou. Times and prices have been cut, and reliability has increased with the improvement in road quality.

Rail freight comes a distant second to road. Woefully neglected for years, China's creaking rail network finally started to receive state funding again in the early 2000s. Not a moment too soon, since the country's rail network carries two huge burdens; it has to transport hundreds of millions of travellers around the country and millions of tons of coal from north-western mines to the power stations that fuel national economic development.

A third option, water transport, dates back to the Grand Canal, first constructed in 5BC and still in use today.[4] Barge transport on inland rivers and canals is slow but cheap and reliable. Levels of pilferage are lower than for rail. Mining companies such as Anglo American have used barges to transport large quantities of earth, sand and lime from quarries.

For those in more of a hurry, the fourth option – air – has grown in popularity with the improvement of the national air infrastructure and the opening up of the airfreight sector to foreign companies. Global players such as Federal Express, DHL and UPS operate express mail delivery nationwide and overseas. A study by Boeing predicts that airfreight from China to the United States will grow at nearly 10% each year, and to Europe at around 9% for the next two decades.

## Distribution: getting goods to market

Under China's command economy, state-owned enterprises (SOEs) traditionally distributed the goods that they manufactured, operating fleets of trucks to transport them directly to the wholesale and retail markets.

These SOEs ran effective monopolies of such commodities and goods as grain, oil, cigarettes and liquor until the mid-1990s, when central government pressure to bring market efficiencies to the state sector forced the SOEs to spin off their distribution activities. These spin-offs were joined by smaller, dynamic private companies seeking to plug the distribution gap in the fast-growing private manufacturing sector. Today, local distributors consist of state-owned companies descended from state-owned – or local city-based monopolies and their spin-offs – and private companies.

### Wholesale markets

Wholesale markets have always played a role in the distribution of goods in modern China, but it was only in the 1980s that they began to increase in size and scale. With growing demands on the country's traditional distribution system, new wholesale markets sprang up around cities and increasingly in remote regions, providing a launching point for goods into the rural market. More than $1 trillion in goods is believed to pass through an estimated 80,000 wholesale markets, including a tiny (but growing) proportion of foreign consumer goods.

Eager to reach beyond China's first- and second-tier cities to third- and fourth-tier markets (and beyond), multinational manufacturers of fast-moving consumer goods have sought to go further than the networks currently offered by distribution companies. Those producing non-perishable goods, in particular, have therefore opted for the wholesale market route, channelling products through the markets in a bid to reach ever more remote regions.

Yet extended access to remote consumer markets comes at the cost of transparency. Once a product reaches the wholesale market, it effectively drops off the radar. Goods may be moved from south to north or east to west by wholesalers seeking to arbitrage regional price differences or exploit more efficient distribution networks in other parts of the country. Without the ability to track their products, marketers cannot accurately assess local demand or regional consumption patterns and preferences. Genuine products may be mixed with counterfeit and copycat goods, which are prevalent in wholesale and smaller local markets. Wholesale markets may open up a company's products to hundreds of millions more potential customers, but with those opportunities come risks that the company must be prepared to accept.

In 2009 the WTO ordered the Chinese government to stop forcing US intellectual property rights owners to deal with only state-run distributors, which are often more expensive than private players. The WTO also told China that it must let foreign companies sell music over the internet, which could help companies such as Apple and its iTunes music-downloading business. The judges said that China had broken a promise it made upon joining the WTO in 2001 to offer relatively open access to foreign mass-produced art: WTO member countries are not permitted to discriminate against imported goods.

Multinational companies have created impressive distribution networks reaching far into the remote regions of the country. Those with the farthest-reaching networks are generally those distributing non-perishable food products. For example, Wrigley has been reaching smaller cities and most rural areas since the 1990s; Instant-noodle and snack-food brands President and Tong Yi can be found in remote villages across the country; Procter & Gamble and Unilever distribute shampoo, soap, laundry powder and other goods in most rural areas. These distribution networks usually comprise several joint ventures or wholly owned logistical operations with provincial or regional coverage that together form a patchwork distribution network spanning most or all of China's consumers. Distribution of foodstuffs, especially perishable foods such as dairy products, relies entirely on the extent and quality of chill- or cold-chain transport networks; these deteriorate as they move into the inland provinces.

As more complex products find their way further inland, the need for after-sales service increases: this presents a greater challenge to multinational companies than distributing the product in the first place.

### Distribution options

With China's growing importance as a global sourcing centre for multinational companies, foreign investors are assessing the entire supply chain. Transport may remain top of the list of concerns, but other factors are also coming into play as the market liberalises and competition increases. Market liberalisation brings greater autonomy and transparency for multinational companies, but also increases competition from foreign and local rivals, often pushing cheaper products into the market (leading to cost-cutting across the supply chain).

- **Keep it in-house.** Nearly one-third of all multinational companies in China – most of them market leaders – have followed the example of China's SOEs and developed their own logistics capabilities. These firms tend to be global operators, such as Procter

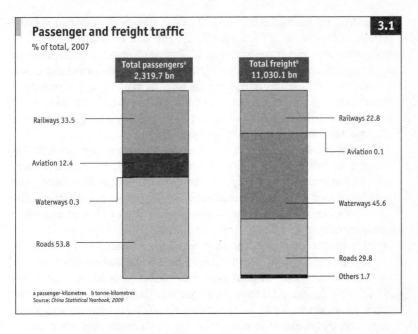

**Passenger and freight traffic**

3.1

% of total, 2007

Total passengers<sup>a</sup>
2,319.7 bn

Total freight<sup>b</sup>
11,030.1 bn

Railways 33.5

Aviation 12.4

Waterways 0.3

Roads 53.8

Railways 22.8

Aviation 0.1

Waterways 45.6

Roads 29.8

Others 1.7

a passenger-kilometres   b tonne-kilometres
Source: *China Statistical Yearbook, 2009*

& Gamble and Nestlé, which have operations sufficiently large to require dedicated distribution networks. These dedicated operations typically take the form of foreign-invested commercial enterprises, which bring far greater transparency to the distribution process.

- **Work with small local partners.** Smaller multinational companies can also work with one or more local distribution firms with comprehensive coverage of specific markets to reach their target consumers. This strategy often requires partnerships with numerous small players and careful planning to create and maintain an effective network. Some of the players can be small, and the competition is abundant, if fragmented. The China Federation of Logistics and Purchasing (CFLP) estimates that there are up to 900,000 logistics firms in China – most of them one-man-and-a-truck operations – compared with 7,000 in the United States.

- **Use third-party logistics providers.** 3PLs offer the most hassle-free option for major multinational companies with substantial volumes (and budgets). They take responsibility for delivering goods from the factory to the customer. According to the CFLP, the market share of China's top ten 3PLs is 13%, and the whole sector is thought to account for roughly 20% of distribution (compared with nearly 60% in the United States and 80% in Japan). In the automotive sector, for example, TNT of the Netherlands and APL Logistics, an US-based unit of Singapore's Neptune Orient Lines, have set up logistics joint ventures with local carmakers. The 3PL market will continue to grow in China. In 2008 YRC Worldwide, a US transport company, acquired a 65% stake in Shanghai Jiayu Logistics, one of the largest local providers of truckload and less-than-truckload services with a fleet of more than 3,000 vehicles. YRC, which has been in the market since 2005, followed its US customers – notably Wal-Mart – to China, and like them is expected to expand its reach beyond Shanghai and into the surrounding Yangtze River Delta region. In 2007, UPS acquired the remaining stake of its local joint-venture partner, Sinotrans.

- **Use agents.** Importers of goods without a manufacturing hub in China can rely on Hong Kong-based trading and distribution firms for a reliable (if costly) route to market. Jebsen has been offering this service in the region for decades; it imported the first Volkswagen Beetle to Hong Kong in 1953. Now it imports luxury goods such as Porsche automobiles from Germany and Raymond Weil watches from Switzerland.

## Obstacles to smooth distribution

- **Hostile geography.** China is a vast country with a difficult terrain. Vast inland mountain ranges have impeded the development of transport and communication networks in central and western regions. In the 1990s, truckers driving west to Lanzhou, capital of western Gansu province, insisted on driving in convoys because of the risk of attacks by wolves when they took rest stops.
- **Underdeveloped networks.** Few distributors have national reach, forcing companies to partner with up to a dozen regional distribution companies in an effort to patch together nationwide distribution networks.
- **Substandard warehousing.** Quality warehousing is hard to find; goods are often kept in poor conditions and warehouses are often not equipped to store specialist products. Inventory is inefficiently monitored leading to oversupply.
- **Opaque supply chain.** Poor tracking capabilities prevent customers from receiving even basic information about which retail outlets sell the most of their products, particularly once goods are sent to wholesale markets. Such is the lack of transparency that multinational consumer-goods firms have been known to

hire staff to identify their products in the market and then trace the route the products took from the factory to the market. Multinational operators are using international technology to help solve the problem. Sam's Club, the US-based bulk discount offshoot of Wal-Mart, has radio-frequency identification (RFID) technology across its China operations, having pushed its suppliers and logistics providers to come on board (or else). RFID technology provides companies with real-time data and instant traceability of goods moving in their supply chain.

## Exporting

China has relied on a booming export-processing capability to drive its economic growth. It was the attractions of cheap land and labour on the mainland that first enticed Hong Kong manufacturers to cut costs by moving their factories across the border into southern Guangdong province. Assembly and low-margin manufacturing fuelled China's development, and there was a surge in exports as goods marked "Made in China" were exported to the United States, Europe and the rest of Asia. The nature of the products made for export has evolved, from garments and toys to domestic appliances and electrical machinery, but the model has not, and steady growth for nearly 30 years has forced China's transport infrastructure to modernise rapidly in a bid to cope with ever-increasing volumes. Exports (both foreign-invested and domestic) will remain an integral part of China's economy for as long as the country continues

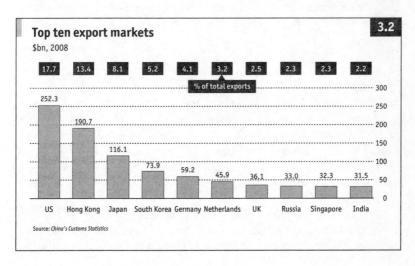

**Top ten export markets** 3.2

$bn, 2008

| 17.7 | 13.4 | 8.1 | 5.2 | 4.1 | 3.2 | 2.5 | 2.3 | 2.3 | 2.2 |

% of total exports

| US | Hong Kong | Japan | South Korea | Germany | Netherlands | UK | Russia | Singapore | India |
| 252.3 | 190.7 | 116.1 | 73.9 | 59.2 | 45.9 | 36.1 | 33.0 | 32.3 | 31.5 |

Source: *China's Customs Statistics*

to offer cheap land and labour, high product quality and an efficient transport infrastructure. All these China currently has and will be able to offer for at least another ten years.

China's main exports zones are also its main regions of growth: the Pearl River Delta in Guangdong and the Yangtze River Delta surrounding Shanghai. In 2007, processed goods accounted for nearly 75% of Guangdong's exports. Even as land and labour costs lose their competitiveness in Guangdong, cheaper manufacturing locations are being found in neighbouring provinces such as Guangxi, Yunnan, Hunan and Jiangxi.

## Market research: beware the data

Information is power, as the saying goes in China, and that presumably includes statistical data. But it does not have to reflect reality. On the contrary, official data have been twisted, massaged and sometimes just plain fabricated – particularly by provincial administrations – to meet whatever purpose was required at the time. The ludicrously inflated grain production figures with which provincial governments sought to win Mao's favour in the Great Leap Forward helped contribute to one of the worst famines in world history, where between 16m and 44m people are believed to have died. Even today, there is a tendency for provincial economic statistics in aggregate to total more than the national figure – a reminder that the ambition of local government officials has not changed over the years. Although the discrepancies are far smaller overall than in the past, and to an extent are only natural when different sources are being used, there remain two notable exceptions: GDP and retail sales, both of which are crucial for foreign investors.

### GDP

In terms of GDP, China started to try to improve its national accounting system in 1985 in order to bring greater accuracy to the process. This included, in 1992, a move away from the old Marxist system of national accounting and the adoption of the system of national accounts (SNA) widely used in other countries. Under the SNA, provincial governments should ideally calculate the amount of goods flowing into and out of their regions; in practice, this is impossible, so this figure is estimated by subtracting total local demand from total local production and seeing what is left.

This finger-in-the-wind method served adequately while the numbers were relatively small, but over the past decade formerly minor discrepancies have become more significant as inter-provincial trade has boomed as a result of improved transport links, the removal of restrictive trade barriers and massive investment by richer coastal provinces in poorer inland ones. Adding to this are the non-standardised methodologies employed by statistics bureaus at the central and local level. Most data estimates are based on the reporting system, which takes its data from company accounts filed with the authorities, but both the National Statistical Bureau and local statistical bodies still rely on surveys to estimate output, and the criteria for such surveys can vary.

### Those retail details

Retail sales data should be taken with particularly large grains of salt. A close inspection of provincial/national data reveals that discrepancies in the primary and tertiary sectors have shrunk since the mid-1990s but those in the secondary sector have grown. The problem is retail sales, which are distorted by two factors, according to Arthur Kroeber of China Economic Quarterly. First, in a hangover from the old Marxist accounting system, retail sales include non-consumer spending (notably government purchases and wholesale spending) but exclude spending on services. Second, retail sales data are typically estimated on a nominal, rather than a real, basis.

As the world waits for China to mature from an investment-fuelled economy to one driven by domestic consumption, retail sales data can present a dangerously inaccurate picture of consumer demand, prompting multinational companies to overestimate the size and growth rate of the market, with damaging consequences. In 2008, for example, according to the data retail sales grew six percentage points faster than urban incomes. The government's explanation for this gap – that households were spending their savings on big-ticket items such as apartments and cars – was not supported by household survey data. The growth in retail sales was more easily attributed to unprecedented government spending in the second half of the year that bolstered the local economy.

### Summary

- **Scale up, not down.** The history of foreign investment in China is littered with examples of multinational companies that entered the mainland market with grandiose plans, only to be forced to scale back or even withdraw completely a few years later. Start small in a small number of cities in one province or region, and get to know the local consumer market – as Wal-Mart did in Guangdong in 1995. Once you have learnt the ropes and understood the idiosyncrasies of the local market, think about expanding into neighbouring provinces or regions.

◪ **Know your customer.** China's consumer market varies hugely according to geography and demography. Make sure your product fits the market. Fast-food companies have had to learn this lesson more swiftly than most. KFC, the largest operator in China, sells Beijing duck-style chicken wraps and *youtiao*, a typically Shanghainese breakfast dish made from fried twisted dough. Meanwhile, Häagen-Dazs sells ice-cream mooncakes (traditional round pastries made from lotus seed paste) during the Mid-Autumn Festival (*Zhongqiujie*).

◪ **Be close to your consumer.** Foreign investors in China typically focus on the three main areas of economic development on the east coast: in the north, the centre and the south. The cities of Beijing, Shanghai and Guangzhou/Shenzhen offer the most attractive starting points for many foreign companies, which can gain experience in the market while being assured of reasonable success in established consumer centres. After securing a foothold in one or more of these markets, companies can choose to expand operations into tier-one cities further inland, many of which offer relatively untapped opportunities. Around the tier-one cities – typically provincial capitals – are fast-growing tier-two and tier-three cities, which (particularly in coastal areas) have improving infrastructure links to make transport and logistics less problematic.

◪ **Consider one of these three distribution models when building a national network.** Work with several regional-level distributors to handle links to urban wholesalers. Directly supply one or more wholesalers in each urban market. Directly supply major retailers (such as supermarket chains or department stores) from the factory.

# 4 Investment risk: dealing with regulations and operational challenges

A conversation with a wise man is better than ten years of study.

Chinese proverb

Membership of the World Trade Organisation (WTO) has liberalised investment structures across numerous sectors, vastly increasing the options for multinational companies. The development of China's legal and tax regimes offers greater protection – and opportunities – for investors, often without the sometimes restrictive need for a local partner. This chapter assesses the benefits and drawbacks of various investment vehicles. Does China's leadership have the capacity – and willpower – to enforce new legislation and to keep improving the regulatory climate?

## The operating environment

Thirty years of open-door investment has given the Chinese government confidence in dealing with foreign investment, and with that confidence has come an easing of restrictions in the shape of constitutional reform. The gradual transition from a planned economy to a system driven by market forces has led to a simplification of business application procedures – though red tape remains a frustration – and stronger protection of property rights and commercial interests. The passing of a private property law in 2007, for example, marks an attempt to reassure China's emerging class of entrepreneurs that their wealth will remain their own.

The biggest step was China's long-awaited accession in 2001 to the WTO, whose members account for 90% of global trade, which has propelled it into the global arena. As China has worked to meet its WTO obligations, the country has naturally matured as an investment destination. Massive inflows of foreign direct investment (FDI) until the second half of 2008 were accompanied by unprecedented fixed-asset investment in infrastructure – notably ports, airports, roads and (after a break of many years) rail – which have helped to ease transport bottlenecks and create a more effective transport network linking coastal provinces with inland regions. The transport system carried a record 188m people by train and 24m people by air during the 2009 Lunar New Year holiday, despite the poor weather that typically affects this holiday season. Meanwhile, state investment in power plants and energy distribution has increased the size of the national power grid, reducing the energy shortages that used to plague businesses in and around major cities.

Restrictions on the size of individual foreign-invested projects in China have also eased, with projects up to $100m no longer needing central government approval provided they do not require state funding. However, Beijing still keeps a close eye on foreign investment and closely controls both its pace and its direction. Investments in most industries are now encouraged, though some sectors or subsectors remain officially "restricted", with stakes limited and central approval required. These include the industries of greatest importance to China's national and economic security: aviation, coal, defence, oil and petrochemicals, power generation and distribution, shipping and telecommunications. According to Li Rongrong, chairman of the State-owned Assets Supervision and Administration Commission (SASAC), a special body directly under the State Council that manages China's state-owned enterprises, the government must keep "absolute control" over SOEs in these sectors and nurture them to become "leading global businesses".

Greater exposure to multinational business operations has also given experience to local officials and the young labour force. Growing numbers of young workers are trained by foreign-invested enterprises, and there is an additional group of Chinese students with an overseas education returning home after graduation.

WTO membership has helped to remove or at least shrink major obstacles to investment. Foreign investor attention has now turned to more specific areas of concern such as intellectual property protection and local protectionism. For the most part, foreign investors are less worried about the overall operating environment and the role of bodies such as ministries and the judiciary, and are more concerned about the things that affect businesses everywhere: competitive pressures from other companies; the rising cost of salaries; and the search for management talent. However, significant investment risks remain. These include red tape, corruption, local protectionism and a potentially alarming propensity to use nationalism as a political and commercial tool. Yet overall, China is improving as an investment destination. According to a World Bank report, *Doing Business 2010*, China came highest of all the BRIC countries in ease of doing business, ranking 89th out of 180 countries – ahead of Russia (120th), Brazil (129th) and India (133rd), but lagging behind regional neighbours Singapore (1st) and Japan (15th).

## Regulatory environment for foreign investment

Since taking the decision to open its doors to foreign investment in 1978, China has worked to strengthen its legal system and create a transparent, rules-based environment for doing business, despite a residual contradiction between efforts to establish a fully fledged legal system and the need for the ruling Communist Party of China (CPC) to retain its dominant position. China's accession to the WTO was followed by a six-year roll-out period during which Beijing systematically opened most of its industries to foreign investment, all the while rapidly introducing or updating essential investment-related laws.

China's ability to shape an effective business environment is far greater than it was three decades ago. It has sufficient experience, talent and know-how in government to simplify and continuously improve the legal system. In 2007–08 alone the government enacted the Bankruptcy Law, the Property Rights Law, the Corporate Income Tax (CIT) law – also known as the Enterprise Income Tax law – the Labour Contract Law and the Anti-Monopoly Law (AML), each one a significant step in China's legal history. It has also ensured greater international buy-in by consulting foreign firms and institutions in the drafting of much legislation. The World Bank and European Union have funded a number of advisory teams to work with the Ministry of Commerce (Mofcom) and other ministries on WTO-compliant legislation. Meanwhile, 16 European and Chinese universities have jointly created the China-EU School of Law (CESL), the first Sino-foreign managed law school, which opened in Beijing's China University of Political Science and Law in 2008. CESL aims to produce lawyers with knowledge of both Chinese and international legal systems. Overall, the number and professional standard of lawyers is rising, with a growing number working in private law firms.

Contradictions and gaps in legislation – mainly caused by an extremely short timeframe and China's lack of legal expertise in some areas – are generally being addressed. Investors' concerns focus more on the ability and willingness of provincial and city authorities to enforce this legislation (see Local protectionism, page 94).

## WTO accession: a tale of endurance

China's relationship with the WTO and its previous incarnation, the General Agreement on Tariffs and Trade (GATT), goes back decades. The Kuomintang government had been one of the original GATT signatories in 1948 but withdrew from the world trade body when it fled to Taiwan in 1949. When China resumed its seat at the UN in 1972, the GATT became the only major world body without China as a member – a diplomatic contradiction that grew more glaring with China's emergence as a global trading power in the 1980s. In 1986, China finally applied for GATT membership, but what would have been a comparatively swift accession process was derailed by the Tian'anmen Square crackdown in 1989 and the subsequent political fallout. Yet China needed GATT membership, not least because it brought with it most-favoured nation status with the United States, by now an important trading partner. During the 1990s there were protracted arguments over China's growing trade surpluses, its status as a "developed" or "developing" nation and a host of other issues. These were ultimately resolved and the country joined the WTO in 2001.

### Improvements under the WTO
A decade on, China has complied with its accession-related requirements and its commercial operating structure is now largely integrated with the WTO framework. Specific improvements include the following:

- **Import tariff cuts.** Most of China's WTO-driven tariff reductions were made by 2007. Since early that year, the general tariff level has stood at 9.8%, with a temporary import tariff rate of 4.2% (lower than the 11% statutory tariff rate) on more than 300 kinds of goods, including natural resource and energy products, in an effort to encourage imports. Car importers, for example, pay standard WTO import tariffs of 25% on imported vehicles but just 10% on auto parts.
- **Liberalisation of restricted sectors.** The Catalogue for the Guidance of Foreign Investment Industries (see below) opens the door to some sectors and shuts it to others. Investing in services and outsourcing is easier – China wants to take market share from India, which has become the leading centre for professional services outsourcing. Investing in sectors that affect national and economic security is restricted.
- **Investment-related legislation.** The introduction in 2007 of the Enterprise Income Tax law, the Labour Contract Law and the Anti-Monopoly Law has helped bring greater transparency and rigour to the operating environment for investors (see Chapter 5).
- **Setting up a business.** It is now easier, safer and cheaper for foreign and domestic investors to set up business in China. The minimum capital requirement for registering a limited liability company is Rmb30,000 ($4,412) – substantially less than the

previous Rmb500,000 ($73,529), though local requirements are sometimes much higher – of which only a portion must be paid upfront, with the balance due over the course of an agreed schedule. According to the World Bank's *Doing Business 2010* report, it takes 14 procedures and 37 days to register a business in China, compared with an average of 8 procedures and 41 days for the East Asia and Pacific region, 13 procedures and 30 days in India, and 9 procedures and 30 days in Russia. To have a greater number of approval procedures than India is a dubious achievement, but more streamlined measures should be introduced in the future.

With WTO membership have come other problems, most of them a consequence of or reaction to China's economic development, such as intellectual property violations (see page 98) and an increase in non-tariff barriers to secure entry to "strategic" industries. As tariffs have been reduced, non-tariff trade barriers and sector-specific restrictions have begun to emerge which foreign investors claim are against the spirit of WTO membership. For instance, vehicle imports are permitted at only four ports (Dalian, Tianjin, Shanghai and Guangzhou Huangpu), forcing importers who previously relied on free-trade zones (also known as bonded zones) to use more costly warehousing facilities. In the financial sector, capital requirements remain prohibitively high for all but the largest players. In agriculture, phytosanitary (food safety and animal and plant health) measures significantly restrict imports. And intellectual property rights remain subject to continual violations despite international pressure for more effective criminal penalties.

## What's encouraged, what's not: the Catalogue for Foreign Investment

The new Catalogue for the Guidance of Foreign Investment Industries lists the sectors in which foreign companies may invest. Updated by the National Development and Reform Commission (NDRC) and Mofcom in 2007, the catalogue lists encouraged, restricted and prohibited sectors (projects not specified in the catalogue are considered permitted).

- ◪ **Encouraged.** High technology, environmental protection, R&D and services industries. The inclusion of the last two categories reflects China's efforts to challenge India, with its strong technical capabilities and English-language fluency, in these areas. Local governments can approve investments of less than $100m;

investments of more than $100m require central government approval (though in practice these are treated favourably). Other officially encouraged categories include agriculture and energy efficiency. As part of its broader economic initiatives, the central government also informally encourages the development of inland regions.

◪ **Restricted.** Heavily polluting industries, property, export-focused manufacturing projects with negligible value-added and resource-thirsty industries. Foreign investors seeking to invest in these industries are likely to need to seek approval from the government. They may increase their chances of success if there are clear incentives for the government, such as job creation or infrastructure development in poorer inland regions. Telecommunications falls into this sector: foreign investors may now take up to a 49% stake in telecoms ventures (with notable exceptions in some internet and telecoms services) anywhere in the country.

◪ **Prohibited.** The relatively short list of industries in which foreign companies cannot (currently) invest includes defence, publishing and others in the broad areas of information, national security and public morality. Also prohibited are foreign investments that target traditional Chinese sectors such as tea and medicine.

Although some categories have moved from encouraged to restricted (notably real estate, where public anger was directed towards foreign developers profiting from increasing property prices at the expense of Chinese people), the general trend is towards opening sectors to foreign investment. In the once heavily restricted banking sector, for example, restrictions on local currency business have been eased to the point where foreign banks can now provide foreign currency and renminbi services to customers in any part of the country, and capital requirements have been reduced to Rmb300m ($44m). In 2007, HSBC, Citibank, Standard Chartered and Bank of East Asia started offering renminbi banking services, focusing on high-end customers. Similarly, liberalisation has reached the insurance sector, with foreign investment now welcome in life, non-life, group, health and pension insurance – though take-up has been slow. Meanwhile, retail, distribution, logistics, manufacturing, tourism and other sectors are free from restrictions.

China's government can impose swift and drastic measures on specific sectors if it chooses to. Growing government concern over the pervasive influence of online games on young users – as well as the poorly regulated nature of the sector – prompted the General Administration of Press and Publication (GAPP), the industry regulator, to prohibit all foreign investment in the Chinese online gaming industry in late 2009. China had 338m internet users as of mid-2009.

### A *cautionary note*
Implementation remains an open question, and one of the main uncertainties for foreign investors will be the ability of the government to control decisions at a provincial and city level. There are a number of areas where the catalogue lacks clarity, raising the question of how foreign investors should act in certain circumstances. In particular, the procedures for approval of investments in restricted categories are unclear; foreign investors applying for large-scale projects, for example, are not sure whether final approval in a restricted category is given by Mofcom, the NDRC, or both. Furthermore, the catalogue's rules often conflict with other investment guidelines. For instance, projects that are "restricted" because they are low-value-added or polluting may have no luck in seeking approval from developed coastal provinces but will be welcomed in the investment-hungry central and western provinces, where the government is keen to encourage foreign investment.

Foreign companies also find that local governments can co-operate in circumventing the central-approval requirement without breaking the rules. Proposed projects can be split into separate phases, each lower than the investment threshold, or they can be handled by different corporate entities within the same investing group. However, although foreign investors may cut down on red tape in the short term, they may encounter problems in the longer term when dealing with central government entities because what is clearly a large-scale investment lacks central approval.

### Transparency and market access
Transparency has always been an issue for foreign investors. An executive who negotiated with Chinese officials in the 1980s said that she often did not know who she was dealing with across the table and who she should be talking to. The absence of published regulations identifying policymakers, regulators and monitors for many sectors only added to the lack of clarity.

China has come a long way in little more than a decade. Few investors in China in the 1990s could have imagined a time when the Chinese government would consult foreign companies before publishing new investment-related legislation. Yet it is usual for business associations such as the European Chamber of Commerce in China to provide feedback on draft regulations through face-to-face meetings with ministry officials. To an extent, this greater transparency is the result of China's WTO obligations and the subsequent creation of the Chinese Government WTO Notification and Consulting Bureau, which require the government to notify the WTO and its members of any changes to laws and regulations in a number of areas, including trade of goods and services, service-related intellectual property rights and foreign exchange control. But there is a practical element to increased co-operation too. China understands that a more inclusive process increases the chances of eliminating glitches in new legislation while also ensuring greater buy-in from foreign business.

### Reducing red tape: the Administrative Licensing Law

For many years the process of setting up a business in China gave foreign investors nightmares. The introduction of the Administrative Licensing Law in 2004 marked a big step towards clarifying investment procedures and the roles and authority of respective official bodies. The law provides formal delineation between government and business, significantly reducing opportunities for official corruption and encouraging government bodies to focus on issues other than making money. The Administrative Licensing Law was part of a ten-year initiative started by the State Council in 2001 to set public administration within a transparent legal framework. A sharp reduction in the number of activities requiring approval or licences has simplified the process and weakened the power of local officials, who used their positions to extract favours, bribes or commercial benefit. Authority to issue licensing rights has also been devolved downwards from central government bodies to industry associations or local agencies.

### Local protectionism

Despite the best efforts of central government, enforcement of regulations at the local level can be patchy – particularly when such regulations are seen as detrimental to local interests. While much of the problem relates to capacity, local protectionism also remains endemic. Particularly in inland areas and smaller towns, local government officials often have stakes in businesses in their area, prompting them to ignore or skirt around central policies that might adversely affect their commercial interests. Even if they are not commercially involved with a local business, local officials will instinctively protect it to maintain tax revenues and employment figures – and often because they simply do not like outsiders. When Hebei-based Sanlu was found to be at the centre of a scandal involving the adulteration of infant formula with melamine in 2008, local officials working in the provincial capital, Shijiazhuang, helped the company attempt to minimise its responsibility for the scandal.

Differences between national and local regulations can also present problems for foreign investors, who may find themselves at a competitive disadvantage in following national rules when up against local companies following local regulations, often with local official support. Contradictions between national and local regulations are less common than in the past, but foreign companies may still find themselves in a situation where to comply with one law could involve breaking another. In such circumstances, foreign companies should take local legal advice and consult with peer companies and trade associations.

Central government protectionist measures can also pose problems for those who export from China or those who rely on imports from China. Although across-the-board sanctions, such as the 27.5% tariff on all Chinese exports proposed in the past by two American senators, Charles Schumer and Lindsay Graham, remain unlikely, smaller-scale protectionist measures targeting specific industries are possible. In 2009, for example, India banned imports of Chinese toys and imposed a tariff on Chinese aluminium imports, and the United States has made a number of complaints to the WTO about Chinese trade policies. The pressure for protectionism has risen internationally as the global economic environment has soured, and although many governments continue to profess strong support for free trade, in practice several have already taken backward steps in this area. Companies should remain aware of the progress of legislation that may affect trade with China, especially in markets that are important to them, and lobby through their own politicians and chambers of commerce against measures that might have a negative impact on their business.

## Investment protection

The risk of expropriation of foreign-invested enterprises (FIEs) is remote. Over the past 30 years the Chinese government has sought to create a business environment with little or no interference at the state level. It can nationalise or expropriate FIEs (including wholly owned foreign enterprises) only in special circumstances, such as when national security interests are threatened. China has signed over 30 informal investment agreements with larger trading nations, eschewing bilateral investment protection treaties except with smaller countries. These bilateral deals typically prohibit expropriation.

However, the low risk of expropriation does not mean that the state cannot and will not exert its power over foreign investors. The state has intervened in some sectors in an effort to steer them in the desired direction for their overall economic development plans. In the steel sector, for example, a number of foreign-invested steel projects were suspended as part of broader government efforts to cool the overheating economy in 2005, and in 2009 four managers of Australian mining company Rio Tinto were detained on charges of stealing state secrets. In 2010 they received jail sentences ranging from seven to 14 years on downgraded charges of bribery and stealing commercial secrets. The detention of the managers (one of them an Australian national) drew worrying comparisons with the Russian authorities' practices.

China is no Russia. Yet government wariness of foreign attempts to acquire significant stakes in what it regards as strategic industries have prompted it to quash a number of major acquisition attempts. In 2007, the NDRC rejected a proposal by Luxembourg-based ArcelorMittal, the world's largest steel producer, to buy a 38.4% stake in Laiwu Steel for $269m on the grounds that the price was too low and the transfer of technology inadequate. (ArcelorMittal instead acquired a 28% stake in steel-products-maker China Oriental Group later that year.) Between 2005 and 2007, Carlyle Group, a US-based private-equity firm, tried unsuccessfully to gain government approval for its acquisition of a stake in Xugong Group Construction Machinery, despite reducing its planned 85% stake purchase to under 36%.

The government has various means at its disposal to limit or reject foreign investments. These include the manipulation of latent xenophobia, which can be fomented on the internet (particularly through blogs and chatrooms) before bursting to the surface in the form of public protests and media hostility, giving the government sufficient grounds to prevent significant foreign acquisitions of national businesses on the grounds of public opposition. Many Chinese are sensitive about foreign ownership because they feel that China's own acquisition efforts overseas have met with nationalist resistance. A notable example is a decision by the US Congress to block the attempted acquisition in 2005 of US company Unocal by CNOOC, a Chinese state-owned oil producer. China's sovereign wealth fund, the China Investment Corp (CIC), continually faces accusations that its acquisitions are strategically rather than commercially motivated. The EU has even suggested that it might block investments by the CIC in strategic sectors because it fears that the CIC is acting purely on the orders of the Chinese government, seeking to serve national interests rather than to gain commercial advantage.

### Foreign investment authorities: national players

Oversight of foreign investment policy is in the hands of roughly five national state agencies, though other entities play a role according to the foreign investor's sector and geographical region. These agencies, all of which have set up departments to deal with WTO-related matters, are as follows:

- Ministry of Commerce (Mofcom), formerly known as the Ministry of Foreign Trade and Economic Co-operation (Moftec) and the Ministry of Foreign Economic Relations and Trade (Mofert), is responsible for drafting regulations governing foreign trade and investment. It also has a monitoring role, vetting all foreign investment projects valued above $30m or falling in the "restricted" category of investments. Within Mofcom, three departments deal with WTO matters: the Department of WTO Affairs, the WTO Notification and Enquiry Centre, and the Fair Trade Bureau for Import and Export. These bodies handle WTO-related issues ranging from trade policies to anti-dumping.
- National Development and Reform Commission (NDRC), formerly the State Planning Commission, is responsible for co-ordinating China's development policies. Its broad remit to develop the macroeconomy gives it authority to restrict foreign investment in particular industries, though this requires consultation with Mofcom and the State Council.
- State Administration for Industry and Commerce (SAIC) issues business licences through its local administration for industry and commerce (AIC) offices. It also deals with trademark inspections and supervises fair competition, dealing with issues such as commercial bribery. In addition, it oversees new industries, such as advertising, which are not under the supervision of any ministry.
- General Administration of Quality Supervision, Entry and Exit Inspection and Quarantine (GAQSIQ) regulates all inspection, quarantine and technical-standard requirements relating to imports and exports.
- State Administration of Tax (SAT). A ministerial-level department under the direction of the State Council, the SAT is responsible for the collection of taxes and enforces the state revenue laws.
- State Administration of Foreign Exchange (SAFE) drafts rules on foreign exchange and manages the state foreign exchange reserves. At the end of June 2009 these stood at $2.1 trillion.

Such attitudes will stoke anti-foreign sentiment in China, where the government has allowed popular protests against foreign embassies or companies. Widespread protests against French companies and brands in China took place in major cities following the disruption of the Olympic torch run through France before the Beijing Olympic Games in 2008. Public protests disrupted operations at Carrefour stores in a handful of cities, with word spreading through internet chatrooms that the retailer supported the Dalai Lama (a rumour it was swift to deny). Anti-foreign protests in China are inevitable as the country struggles to find its place in the international community, but they usually pass relatively quickly. Foreign investors and their staff and families in China should aim to keep a low profile and work with government missions to help ease tensions.

## Protecting intellectual property

Poor protection of intellectual property (IP) remains the largest single deterrent to multinational companies considering an investment in the mainland market. The United States Trade Representative's Special 301 Report on global IP violations for 2009 remarked that the enforcement of IP rights in China "remains largely ineffective and non-deterrent". According to US government data, China-made products account for 81% of all counterfeit goods seized in the United States in 2008 (compared with 80% in 2007), and US seizures of counterfeit goods from China increased 40% in value year-on-year. Meanwhile, 53% of all counterfeit imports into Europe in 2008 came from China (compared with 58% in 2007).

Within China, well over half the consumer goods in daily use are believed to be counterfeit. Although counterfeiting is still endemic, there has been a marked improvement in legislation and enforcement over the past five years; counterfeiting of daily-use goods was believed to be as high as 90% in 2004. This marked improvement is partly because of require-ments under the WTO's Trade-Related Aspects of Intellectual Property Rights (TRIPS), relentless international pressure and a growing need for protection on the part of emerging indigenous national brands. China has implemented a host of new laws and regulations since joining the WTO in a bid to strengthen its intellectual property rights regime. These include new or spruced-up versions of the trademark, patent, copyright and pharmaceuticals laws.

Table 4.1 **Where software piracy is highest, % of software pirated**

| Country | 2005 | 2006 | 2007 | 2008 |
|---|---|---|---|---|
| Georgia | – | – | – | 95 |
| Bangladesh | – | – | 92 | 92 |
| Armenia | 95 | 95 | 93 | 92 |
| Zimbabwe | 90 | 91 | 91 | 92 |
| Sri Lanka | – | – | 90 | 90 |
| Azerbaijan | 94 | 94 | 92 | 90 |
| Moldova | 96 | 94 | 92 | 90 |
| Yemen | – | – | 89 | 89 |
| Libya | – | – | 88 | 87 |
| Pakistan | 86 | 86 | 84 | 86 |
| Venezuela | 82 | 86 | 87 | 86 |
| Indonesia | 87 | 85 | 84 | 85 |
| Vietnam | 90 | 88 | 85 | 85 |
| Iraq | – | – | 85 | 85 |
| Ukraine | 85 | 84 | 83 | 84 |
| Algeria | 83 | 84 | 84 | 84 |
| Montenegro | 83 | 82 | 83 | 83 |
| Paraguay | 83 | 82 | 82 | 83 |
| Cameroon | 84 | 84 | 84 | 83 |
| Nigeria | 82 | 82 | 82 | 83 |
| Zambia | 83 | 82 | 82 | 82 |
| Bolivia | 83 | 82 | 82 | 81 |
| Guatemala | 81 | 81 | – | 81 |
| China | 86 | 82 | 82 | 80 |
| El Salvador | 81 | 82 | 81 | 80 |

Source: Business Software Alliance, IDC

However, the problem, as in so many emerging markets, is one of enforcement. China's enforcement bodies lack the funding, credibility and incentive to act against violators, and close links to local administrations and companies can create conflicts of interest. Enforcement bodies have no powers of arrest and cannot rely on local police forces, which are often colluding with counterfeiters. Furthermore, the relatively light penalties for infringements fail to deter.

Table 4.2 **Chinese customs' seizures of counterfeit goods**

| Year | Value (Rmb m) | No. of seizures |
|------|--------------|----------------|
| 1999 | 92.0 | 225 |
| 2000 | 56.7 | 295 |
| 2001 | 134.9 | 330 |
| 2002 | 95.6 | 573 |
| 2003 | 68.0 | 756 |
| 2004 | 84.2 | 1,051 |
| 2005 | 99.8 | 1,210 |
| 2006 | 203.0 | 2,473 |
| 2007 | 438.8 | 3,310 |
| 2008 | 300.0[a] | – |

a Estimate.
Source: State Intellectual Property Office, General Administration of Customs

Table 4.3 **Court hearings of IPR-related lawsuits**

| Year | No. of lawsuits |
|------|----------------|
| 2004 | 9,329 |
| 2005 | 13,424 |
| 2006 | 14,219 |
| 2007 | 17,877 |
| 2008 | 24,406 |

Source: State Intellectual Property Office

As well as toothless enforcement agencies, numerous other factors contribute to rampant counterfeiting in China:

☑ **Economic liberalisation.** In China's booming free market, local entrepreneurs are constantly searching for goods to copy or counterfeit, either for export or for the domestic market.

◪ **Fragmented regulatory environment.** Responsibility for enforcing IP legislation is split among government bodies. The State Intellectual Property Office (SIPO) is responsible for implementing IP legislation overall, but other bodies involved in the task include the State Administration of Industry and Commerce (SAIC), the General Administration of Quality Standards, Inspection and Quarantine (GAQSIQ), the Ministry of Public Security (MPS) and the General Administration of Customs (GAC, or Customs).

◪ **Substandard judiciary.** Inexperienced, biased judges can make local courts an unpleasant experience for multinational companies, especially in central and western regions where there are close relationships among the judiciary, local government, party and state-owned business.

◪ **Low prosecution rate.** Criminal prosecutions for piracy are rare, largely because of under-empowered enforcement agencies, poor judicial quality and legal inconsistencies. Some improvements have been detected since 2004 when the Supreme People's Court issued guidelines for criminal liability standards in counterfeiting cases.

◪ **Light penalties.** Counterfeiting in China offers entrepreneurs huge profits without the threat of substantial penalties such as crippling fines or lengthy imprisonment. The value of goods, and consequently fines, is assessed at too low a level to put pirates out of business, enabling them to start up again with a new venture, possibly in a new location.

### Pirates act with impunity

The consequence is that local entrepreneurs who would otherwise be contributing positively to national economic development are attracted to counterfeit production and protect their businesses in highly creative ways. Some bring counter suits in legal cases against them; others evade detection through just-in-time distribution models and sophisticated warehousing systems, storing counterfeit inventory at numerous locations. Entire villages and communities may be employed in the manufacture of certain counterfeit products, with the local area monitored by surveillance cameras and patrolled by guards, and local residents wary of any outsiders who might threaten the factory that is providing employment for them, their families and their neighbours. It is not surprising, then, that local enforcement teams attempting to raid factories in such locations are forced to retreat in the face of hundreds of angry residents prepared to use physical violence.

### Lobby groups

In an attempt to increase pressure on central government to strengthen IP rights, foreign companies formed the Quality Brands Protection Committee (QBPC) in 2000. Registered under the auspices of the China Association of Enterprises with Foreign Investment (CAEFI), the QBPC had 184 members with combined foreign investments in China of more than $30 billion as of 2009. A range of sectors are represented: consumer electronics (Philips), sporting apparel (Nike), personal computers (Compaq), confectionery (Mars), personal care (Procter & Gamble) and carbonated soft drinks (Coca-Cola). Smaller groups lobby for foreign companies in particular sectors. They include the Federation for Research-based Pharmaceutical Industries Association (FRPIA) and the Automotive Industry Working Group (AIWG), set up in 2004. The AIWG is an alliance of international carmakers and auto parts manufacturers, with members including Caterpillar, DaimlerChrysler, Denso Corp, General Motors, Robert Bosch and Volkswagen.

### IP protection

Foreign investors seeking to protect their IP should consider the following measures:

- **Register trademarks and patents.** Trademarks (in both Chinese and English) that a company wishes to protect should be registered in China, possibly even before they are used there, to deter competitors. Viktor Arak, CEO China at Eriez Magnetics, was previously group legal counsel for Electrolux in Asia. He recalls that trademark piracy was a major headache for Electrolux because its brand name – like every well-known trademark in China – is typically registered in numerous categories by small businesses seeking to leverage brand awareness, albeit in relation to a different product. Thus the Electrolux brand name was registered for car headlights, shampoo and underwear. These applications would normally be blocked in the West, but in China the trademark office is overwhelmed with some 700,000 applications (in Chinese and English), making independent screening impossible.
- **Invest in physical – and information – security design.** By working with

a security design company in planning facilities and installing effective information technology systems, foreign investors can control the flow of IP around their sites and so minimise the risk of IP theft. These measures also ensure traceability in the event of an IP leak, enabling IP owners to improve their controls. Restricting employees' access to confidential information to only that which they need to use can be effective.

- **Train staff.** Educating staff and raising their awareness of IP protection strategies is crucial. Consider bringing in external consultants to drive the message home. Carry out random IP security audits to ensure staff are adhering to IP protection guidelines.
- **Join lobby groups.** Foreign companies can achieve more as a group in lobbying government ministries and official trade associations for tougher anti-piracy measures, although the process will be a long one. The Beijing-based QBPC is a predominantly international and consumer goods-focused association of more than 120 companies which lobbies central government for tougher IP policy. Specialist associations also exist within important industries such as pharmaceuticals.
- **Share IP protection advice with local companies.** Chinese companies are not immune to IP infringements. Foreign investors can win trust and support by helping local companies with emerging brands to develop their own IP protection plans.
- **Don't bring in the best without stringent IP protection measures.** Do not bring in high value-added and core competency processes unless you have adequate information security measures in place.
- **Practise what you preach.** Foreign investors should also be aware that Chinese companies target foreign firms that infringe domestically registered IP rights. A typical example is the use of pirated software (often unknowing) on office systems. Regularly audit your software systems.

IP enforcement is always an option, though putting the genie back in the bottle can be difficult. According to its manager, one local investigations company typically carries out more than 1,000 raids a year, mainly for multinational consumer goods brands. Local companies producing copycat goods can be virtually impossible to deal with. Major foreign brands faced with niggling competition have historically resorted to acquiring such companies – a solution that the owners of such companies had always aimed for. Of the eight local cola manufacturers that emerged after the arrival of Coca-Cola in the early 1980s, seven had been taken over by foreign partners by the mid-1990s, including most notably Tianfu Cola (the first local rival to Coca-Cola), which was acquired by Pepsi in 1994.

## Product safety

In 2007–08 a spate of safety scandals involving Chinese products and food caused frictions both abroad and at home. Pet food, toothpaste, car tyres, toys, seafood, vegetables and dairy products were some of the categories affected. Pressure from international trading partners was a source of concern for the Chinese government, which signed a new product safety memorandum of understanding with Europe and the United States at the first high-level summit on product safety and traceability in Brussels in 2008. It also introduced new legislation following a huge public outcry over a series of scandals involving contaminated foods, though delays in implementing the long-awaited Food Safety Law, which took effect in 2009, aroused further public anger. In a number of cities, including Beijing, local authorities introduced product and food safety campaigns.

Multinational retailers generally comply with (or far exceed) product and food safety standards, though local authorities can subject them to particularly close scrutiny in a bid to deflect criticism of local companies. Multinational companies use public attention to food safety to their advantage. Wal-Mart, for example, has run "food safety month" programmes to highlight its international-standard food safety measures.

### Consumer protection

As food and product safety issues have found their way into the media, consumer consciousness has increased and an increasingly vocal body of consumer champions has emerged in opposition to fake and shoddy products. Shenzhen-based *Southern Metropolitan News*, an independent newspaper, is known as a champion of consumer rights. Chinese consumers even mark World Consumer Rights Day (March 15th). A worrying 19% of products for domestic consumption failed to meet quality and safety standards in the first half of 2007, according to the GAQSIQ – albeit lower than the nearly 22% figure reported in 2006.

Popular pressure on the government also ensured the amendment in 2009 of the 1994 Consumer Protection Law, giving greater power to the state-backed China Consumers' Association (CCA), which can now appear in court on behalf of consumers rather than just mediating between consumers and vendors before court proceedings. The CCA's 3,100 branches received nearly 648,000 complaints from 4.4m consumers in 2008, leading to the recovery of Rmb66m ($9.7m) through measures such as refunds and product recalls. Foreign companies are occasionally involved in consumer disputes, which inevitably make local or national headlines. In 2009 a university student sued Coca-Cola for violations of labour laws after he was allegedly beaten by staff at an employment agency hiring for Coca-Cola's bottling plant in eastern Zhejiang province.

## Crisis management and business continuity planning

As multinational companies increase their dependence on China, the importance of planning for potential disruptions to their sourcing and supply chain operations becomes critical. Companies with China operations need to create and maintain contingency plans to ensure business continuity and effective duty of care. Customised crisis management planning and training enables companies to anticipate incidents and keep the initiative when such incidents occur. Potential crises fall into the following categories.

### Environmental

- **Environmental disasters.** These are officially the responsibility of the company in question. The government has demonstrated its commitment to environmental protection through the upgrading of the State Environmental Protection Administration to a ministry (the Ministry of Environmental Protection, or MEP) in 2008. Enforcement remains patchy, but the MEP keeps a close eye on foreign companies. Even those with strong programmes in place should be prepared to handle any negative publicity in this respect.
- **Natural disasters.** The worst natural disaster in recent history was the Sichuan earthquake in 2008, which killed nearly 90,000 people and destroyed 80% of the buildings at the epicentre in the south of the province. Transport and communications to the region were cut and additional resources were diverted to the rescue operation, thereby affecting business operations elsewhere in the province.
- **Weather.** In recent years central and southern provinces have suffered from freak snowstorms in January and February, causing transport systems to break down as millions of travellers head home for the Chinese New Year public holiday. Seemingly minor disruptions can have far-reaching consequences; for instance, rail freight delays have prevented coal reaching power stations, leading to local power cuts.

## Health and safety

- **Pandemics and medical emergencies.** Pandemics such as SARS, avian flu and H1N1 pose a serious threat to businesses, particularly multinational businesses with far-reaching supply chains and a growing reliance on China both as producer and consumer.
- **Safety standards.** National safety standards for buildings in China are much lower than in western countries. Foreign companies should carry out regular engineering checks to ensure building safety, and should fully brief and drill staff on evacuation plans.
- **Traffic accidents.** Traffic accidents involving company executives are regarded as the most common disruption to daily business operations in China.
- **Workplace accidents and abuse.** Foreign companies should have crisis communication plans to deal with employee accidents in the workplace. They should also have a clear set of minimum labour standards, for their own facilities and for subcontractors, covering underage workers and appropriate payment of wages. Efforts should be made to ensure that these standards are not abused.

## Political and legal

- **Extortion and product contamination.** Employees (current or former) with grievances or seeking to make money occasionally resort to extortion or production contamination.
- **Kidnap or detention by the local authorities, missing persons.** Although kidnap for ransom is rare in China, the number of incidents involving local nationals is growing; detentions by the local authorities generally take place in cities away from the coast and are usually related to business disputes with state-owned enterprises linked to the local government.
- **Labour unrest, including armed or violent attacks on employees, facilities or management.** Labour unrest has increased sharply in recent years, fuelled partly by a widening income gap between rich and poor, persistent corruption in the state sector, and widespread factory closures caused by more stringent product safety regulations and falling export demand following the 2008 financial crisis.
- **Political or civil unrest.** Political demonstrations or protests are almost always localised, though they can turn violent as protesters vent their frustrations over, for example, official corruption. Anti-foreign demonstrations (sometimes sanctioned by the authorities) can be more widespread and co-ordinated, usually resulting from diplomatic incidents. Such demonstrations are, however, rarely violent and are carefully controlled by the authorities.
- **Reputation.** Scandals can damage the reputation of the foreign company involved, both abroad and within China, where the local media are often keen to find stories that portray foreign companies in a poor light – partly to encourage

others to raise their standards. For example, in mid-2009 Apple was embroiled in a controversy when a Chinese employee of one of its subcontractors, Taiwan's Foxconn, committed suicide. Newspaper reports suggested that Foxconn security staff had used inappropriate methods when interrogating the employee over a suspected theft.

Desktop training and simulation exercises help companies select the right crisis management team (not necessarily the chief executive who travels all the time or the chief financial officer who wants to take control) and give the team the confidence and guidance to manage incidents. The aim of such planning is to develop processes to help manage incidents and minimise their potential impact on company operations (and reputation). Dom Chester, crisis management practice leader at Control Risks, a risk consultancy, believes that effective planning enables companies to respond in an organised, timely and effective way to major incidents posing significant risks to the safety of their personnel, the success of their operations and the integrity of their reputation.

## Closures and exiting businesses

Foreign investors in China may face added legal and regulatory risks as the economic downturn forces them to take actions that could be avoided in better times. Shedding labour, closing factories and liquidating businesses are heavily regulated processes in China. Firms that fail to follow appropriate procedures may face lawsuits from employees and sanctions by the authorities; and those that break the law may find their ability to operate in China severely constrained. Foreign firms are likely to be especially vulnerable, as they often lack the political connections necessary to operate in the legal grey areas that some Chinese firms can exploit. Nevertheless, it is often possible to negotiate agreements with local authorities that incur less expense than a strict adherence to the regulations, especially if the potential for future expansion can be emphasised. Foreign businesses seeking to cut operations in China should consult lawyers to make sure they are fully aware of their legal responsibilities and the options available.

### Bankruptcy law

China's Enterprise Bankruptcy Law took effect in 2007. The law, which took 12 years to draft, governs the bankruptcy of both state-owned enterprises (SOEs) and private business. It gives greater protection to creditors and recognises overseas proceedings, which is important for cross-border insolvency issues. Significantly, the law also includes civil or even criminal liability for the directors, supervisors and senior officers of the bankrupt company if they are deemed to have failed in certain duties or made specific mistakes. Between 2005 and 2008, the State-owned Assets Supervision and Administration Commission allowed more than 2,100 SOEs to go bankrupt, compared with some 3,660 between 1994 and 2005. China dismantled 31,000 of its SOEs (including those that were allowed to go bankrupt) in the period 2003–07, a reduction of 20.7%.

### Law firms: going with the flow

Since the global economic crisis slowed down the flow of deals into China, mainland-based lawyers have found themselves doing different things. Gone are the days of arbitration; in has come dispute resolution. One Australian lawyer who has worked in Shanghai since the 1990s reckons that he spends more time on dispute resolution cases – more often than not contract defaults – than he does on arbitration. This is a new departure for China, where a traditional distaste for confrontational litigation has meant that problems are solved through arbitration and out-of-court settlements. Indeed, contracts between foreign companies and their local partners typically contain a detailed clause covering arbitration provisions.

However, as domestic companies have grown in size, number and competitiveness, the aversion to legal wrangling has shrunk, with more and more Chinese companies now prepared to embark on bitter and prolonged legal battles in court. What is more, international companies are increasingly turning to local companies in litigation cases, in part because they appear to gain comfort from having local support in unfamiliar legal surroundings. This also goes some way towards assuaging foreign perceptions of bias towards Chinese partners.

Local law firms are likely to make further headway in areas such as litigation, helped not only by the growing demand for litigation but also by the traditional reliance of international law firms in China on easier (and more lucrative) transactional work: mergers and acquisitions, investments and project finance. Foreign lawyers have faced restrictions in practising local law, but the proportion of litigation work taken on by international law firms is expected to increase gradually as more local lawyers join big-name practices, even after strong transactional deal flows return.

However, foreign companies should not rely on the bankruptcy process, since Chinese law courts may prevent foreign companies from exercising their rights if they are deemed to be against the interests of the local party. China's courts are not yet fully geared up to hear complex bankruptcy cases, since they lack the training and experience, and when they will be is unclear. Ghislain de Mareuil, a Shanghai-based corporate partner at DLA Piper, an international law firm, advises companies to opt for restructuring outside court if possible, since in a court case an administrator is appointed and control over the company is effectively lost.

### The judiciary and foreign investors

China's judiciary has improved in quality and grown in size over the past ten years, but it continues to lack independence and objectivity, with many judges being ex-military officers or from the local community. In smaller jurisdictions away from the major cities, impartiality is particularly difficult. Many foreign-invested enterprises prefer to settle out of court or seek international arbitration rather than taking disputes to local courts.

Change is coming slowly, however, helped by a growing need on the part of local plaintiffs for fair court hearings in matters such as IP rights. In 2008, the success of a Shanghai-based company in suing a local download service provider prompted six US film companies to follow suit. Foreign investors are advised to avoid legal action if possible by developing and maintaining cordial links with neighbours and business partners, and to double check the validity of all Chinese-language legal documentation. They should be aware that courts in coastal cities have greater experience of dealing with foreign companies and are likely to grant a relatively fair hearing, and that wholly owned foreign enterprises eliminate the risk of legal disputes with a joint-venture partner. Should foreign companies be obliged to seek arbitration, they should work with law firms in doing so. See Appendix 4 for a list of international law firms with well-developed arbitration experts in China.

### Summary

- **China is no Russia.** Investment protection is improving. The threat of nationalisation or expropriation remains small. China will continue to maintain as attractive an investment environment as possible.
- **Regulations are one thing, enforcement another.** The central government has introduced dozens of major new laws over the

past decade in a bid to build a robust legal framework based on international standards. These efforts have been impressive, but problems remain with enforcement – thanks in part to local protectionism, insufficient investment in provincial regulatory bodies and a poor (though improving) judiciary.

# 5 Setting up: corporate structures and tax issues

It doesn't matter whether the mice are white or black as long as they avoid the cat.

A modern twist on Deng Xiaoping's oft-quoted phrase[1]

**M**embership of the WTO has liberalised investment structures in numerous sectors, vastly increasing the options for multinational companies. The development of China's legal and tax regimes offers greater protection – and opportunities – for investors, often without the sometimes restrictive need for a local partner. This chapter assesses the benefits and drawbacks of various investment vehicles. Does China's leadership have the power – and willpower – to enforce new legislation and to keep improving the regulatory climate?

## Corporate structures

For many years, the only way for foreign investors to gain access to the Chinese market was in the form of a joint venture. China had gained experience of joint ventures in the 1950s through contracts with other state-run partners in the Soviet bloc. Chipolbrok, modern China's first joint venture between Polish and Chinese shipping brokers set up in the early 1950s, is now a highly successful business. Since then, hundreds of thousands of joint ventures have been created with varying proportions of foreign ownership.

In the old days, the problem was how to find decent partners. Some foreign investors were lucky in their choice of partners in these early Sino-foreign equity joint ventures; others were unlucky or simply failed to do their due diligence. Happily there is now more choice, except for those investing in certain industry categories. Foreign investors officially can opt for any of four basic company structures, as defined by Chinese law: joint ventures, wholly owned foreign enterprises (WOFEs), holding companies and joint-stock companies. They can also opt not to set up companies but instead to operate representative or branch offices of their own entities, though these are restricted in what they can do.

Although WOFEs are the preferred investment vehicle for foreign investors, mergers and acquisitions have become a popular means of entering the market or expanding existing operations quickly and effectively (see Chapter 6). WTO membership has opened up dozens of sectors such as advertising, logistics, hotels and engineering, but many others still restrict foreign investors to joint-venture operations, such as finance, telecoms, publishing, automotives and mining. Local joint-venture partnerships for foreign investors operating in highly regulated industries can bring simplicity and efficiency to business procedures.

Table 5.1 **Changes in foreign direct investment channels**

| | 2000 | 2001 | 2002 | 2003 | 2004 | 2005 | 2006 | 2007 | 2008 |
|---|---|---|---|---|---|---|---|---|---|
| Total FDI[a] ($ billion) | 40.7 | 46.9 | 52.7 | 53.5 | 60.6 | 60.3 | 63.0 | 74.8 | 92.4 |
| Joint ventures (%) | 35.3 | 33.6 | 28.4 | 28.8 | 27.0 | 20.2 | 20.5 | 18.9 | 18.7 |
| Co-operative ventures (%) | 16.2 | 13.3 | 9.6 | 7.2 | 5.1 | 2.5 | 2.8 | 1.7 | 2.1 |
| Foreign enterprises (%) | 47.3 | 50.9 | 60.2 | 62.4 | 66.4 | 59.4 | 67.2 | 69.3 | 78.3 |
| Foreign-invested share holding enterprises (%) | 0.3 | 1.1 | 1.3 | 0.6 | 1.3 | 1.2 | 0.6 | 0.6 | 0.9 |
| Co-operative development (%) | 0.9 | 1.1 | 0.5 | 0.1 | 0.2 | 0.0 | 0.0 | 0.0 | 0.0 |
| Others (banking, insurance and securities) (%) | 0.0 | 0.03 | 0.0 | 0.9 | 0.03 | 16.7 | 8.9 | 9.5 | 0.0 |

a Non-financial.
Sources: CEIC; Ministry of Commerce

## Wholly owned foreign enterprises

The advent of WOFEs in China was a great relief to foreign investors who had spent many years struggling with joint-venture partners. Over the past decade, the approval rate for WOFEs has been much quicker than that for joint ventures.

WOFEs are governed by the Law of the PRC on Enterprises Operated Exclusively with Foreign Capital (1986, amended 2000) and its implementing rules (1990, amended 2001), and the Company Law (2006), which details those unrestricted sectors in which foreign investors can set up WOFEs. Released from the restrictions of having to partner with local companies, foreign companies have turned to WOFEs in their thousands, either as first-time entrants or choosing to buy out their local partners to gain full ownership and control.[2]

### Advantages
- Total control over management.
- IP protection.
- Free choice of location.
- Easy to set up.
- Easy to terminate (joint ventures need agreement from both parties to liquidate).

### Disadvantages
- Local officials may dislike WOFEs as there is no partnership with a local firm.
- No local mentor to guide and protect if necessary.
- Cannot list locally.

## Joint ventures: horses for courses

The joint venture may be down, but it is not out. A Beijing-based executive says:

> For many companies and industries, joint ventures are still very much in mode, especially in the restricted sectors such as insurance and health. In these sectors it's not yet possible to take over 100% and so the trick is to ensure you have the right partner and endeavour to align the partners' strategies and long-term goals. If you get that part right, you can have a smooth partnership. Get it wrong and you might find yourself on the losing side of a joint-venture legal battle, fought in the Chinese courts. Certainly joint ventures are a company's access to the Chinese market. In these situations the foreign party might be willing to take a minority stake in a joint venture to gain experience in the Chinese market and test the waters before going into a larger investment on their own.

China has two basic forms of joint venture: equity and contractual. As is the case elsewhere, equity joint ventures involve dividing profits among partners according to the proportion of their equity stakes. In China it is common for the local partner to contribute non-cash equity, typically property, equipment and land. By contrast, contractual joint ventures distribute profits according to what is agreed in the joint-venture contract. This model, which is much less common, is sometimes found in larger-scale infrastructure projects.

Joint ventures offer the only route for foreign investors in some industries. A local partner can provide a number of advantages: a local distribution network, a recognised local brand, access to land and (though these are often exaggerated) *guanxi* or valuable connections (see Chapter 1, page 17). At the same time, joint ventures are generally less flexible than WOFEs and inadequately structured to allow for easy expansion; this frequently leads to conflict between the partners, exacerbated by different management and business cultures. As the environment for WOFEs continues to expand, more and more foreign investors are turning their backs on the joint venture.

The aim of a joint venture is to find a local partner to help fill gaps or minimise weaknesses in a company's China strategy. It serves as a means to an end, acting as a vehicle to help achieve the company's overall China strategy. For example, large-scale, complex projects may require partnerships with major state-owned players because of the impact they may have on provincial or national economic interests. In the old days, foreign investors thought themselves lucky if their joint-venture partner was happy to remain largely silent and detached from business operations. That view has changed as the need for real input from local partners has increased and their competence has generally grown stronger. Multinational investors now select partners who have the strengths they need – government relations, industry experience, distribution networks and consumer base – to contribute actively and positively to the partnership.

The Economist Intelligence Unit's Elizabeth Cheng believes that although many sectors have opened to foreign investments, having a local partner or partners remains important in terms of network building, smoothing processes in bureaucratic corridors, nailing down competitive resources and other functions. She says:

> The areas that least need a joint venture partner are probably in OEM manufacturing and retailing. Where there are substantial profit margins to be made, you can be sure that there are many

*local vested interests who will give you a very hard time if you cut them out.*

### Do your due diligence

Due diligence is crucial when considering the information provided by independent third parties and that given by local companies, local partners and their affiliates. Before entering a joint venture partnership:

- **Research your partners.** Foreign investors entering into joint ventures with local partners should proceed with caution, giving themselves time to carry out extensive due diligence. Gather information on the existing plant and manufacturing capability, labour force, depth of management quality, suppliers and customers.
- **Check reputation and integrity.** External consultants offer due diligence of all kinds: financial due diligence by the Big Four (and other) accounting firms; legal due diligence by any number of international and local law firms; and "reputational" due diligence, which assesses the professional reputation, business networks and overall integrity of key principals. China's traditionally opaque business environment makes it difficult for foreign investors to get a true feel of whether a proposed joint-venture partner is the right one or not. Local government officials and investment zone authorities may try partnering your company with a loss-making state-owned enterprise: due diligence can reveal entities which are basket cases. More often than not, problems arise not with a joint-venture partner's tangible assets and liabilities or even its intangible assets such as management quality, technical expertise, distribution networks and government *guanxi*, but with clashes in personalities and an insufficient understanding of the aims and motives of the local partner. (See Chapter 8 for a more detailed analysis.)
- **Understand and trust each other.** Misunderstanding of the real meaning of the contract plagues many potentially fruitful relationships between foreign investors and local Chinese companies because there simply has been no meeting of minds – notwithstanding the execution of contracts. The most effective method of ensuring understanding between the parties is to negotiate the terms of an agreement and, once the contract is drafted, review the document term by term and confirm consensus and understanding of each one. This is obviously best done with translators for each side. This step may appear to be tedious and unnecessary, but it may save the investor much disappointment, and even financial loss, later. Local partners must confirm all promises and guarantees.

They must agree to abide by every step of the national – as well as provincial – laws. This can be tricky when local or provincial pledges contradict national rules and policies.

◪ **Use your common sense.** There are countless stories of foreigners arriving in China and somehow forgetting their business sense – and common sense too. Chinese business culture may differ substantially from your home country, but basic principles hold true. Pay attention to gut feelings. If you sense risk in a potential venture, trust your instinct.

◪ **Take your time.** The most valuable commodity for foreign investors seeking to enter China is time. No aspect of partnering should be rushed. At the right time (when the relationship is developing), senior management from the foreign company should visit China to meet their senior counterparts and give their impression of the market and potential partner. China is not unique. It may seem like another planet to visiting foreign executives, but similar business principles apply.

◪ **Never underestimate your partners.** In his book *The China Dream*, Joe Studwell warns against underestimating Chinese partners and the difficulties of obtaining a foothold in China.

## Holding companies

The holding company model offers advantages to larger multinationals with a number of investments in China, enabling them to consolidate all their entities under a corporate umbrella, which becomes the main shareholder in all those companies. More than 250 holding companies – usually WOFEs, though joint ventures with local partners can make sense if the partner in question controls essential sales and distribution networks – are currently in operation in China. Having central control of all China projects through a single controlling entity gives corporate headquarters peace of mind and allows it to focus on saving costs (by consolidating functions such as human resources, for example) and developing national strategy. Multinationals with holding companies in China include General Electric, Motorola, Philips, Siemens and Unilever. A group finance company, a variant based on the holding company model but with greater financial autonomy, enables multinational investors to provide financial services to their subsidiaries in China. However, this structure is complex and requires heavy capital commitments, making it less popular than the holding company model.

## The office option

### Representative offices

For many companies seeking to get a foothold in China in the 1980s and 1990s, representative offices offered the best option. This approach still offers benefits for companies, particularly those in the services sector. Manufacturers may use a representative office as a starting point to assess local market conditions and opportunities before investing in a WOFE or joint venture. Many companies still maintain representative offices, and if they are able to operate from outside China but need a minimal presence in the country, this is still a reasonable way of doing so. John Williams believes the representative office is still a good vehicle for managing corporate affairs, marketing research and other activities.

Representative offices offer advantages for foreign investors entering China. They are fairly easy and cheap to approve and set up – and much less painful than a joint venture or WOFE to shut down. But the authorities now tax income from representative offices on a "deemed-income" basis (despite the fact that such offices are not supposed to be income-generating) in recognition of the fact that they typically facilitate sales in the country even if the work is done elsewhere. New regulations issued by the State Administration of Taxation (SAT) in February 2010 added further restrictions to representative offices in China; more can be expected to follow.

Other advantages of representative offices are that they can:

- liaise with potential and existing clients;
- research the market on behalf of its parent company;
- carry out research and produce data for potential clients;
- co-ordinate the China activities of the parent company;
- act as a consultant, with billing taking place overseas.

But they have limitations. They cannot:

- carry out for-profit work;
- sign contracts on behalf of the parent company;
- represent any company other than the parent company;
- invoice clients or collect money for services or products.

### Branch offices

Unlike representative offices, branch offices may conduct business. All foreign-invested enterprises (FIEs) can set up branch offices by obtaining a separate business licence from the SAIC, though the scope of business must be the same as the parent company. Branches are most popular with non-manufacturing businesses, notably financial services such as banking. This applies particularly to international banks, because when the sector was still heavily restricted in the 1990s and early 2000s they were required to set up branch offices in Lujiazui, Pudong's financial district, to qualify for business licences.

## Tax environment

The unification of corporate tax rates for domestic and foreign enterprises has removed previous long-running sources of uncertainty. Nevertheless, China's tax rates remain high by international standards, and given rising demands for public expenditure to improve the country's social welfare net, the overall tax burden will stay high for companies. Moreover, local government finances are chaotic; many regions suffer chronic deficits and have resorted to levying ad hoc charges and fees, sometimes of dubious legality, raising the effective tax burden. Some local governments are also known to offer tax incentives that breach central guidelines. Foreign firms that have unwittingly breached tax regulations may, in future years, face bills for back taxes due.

Unification of the dual tax-rate system for FIEs and local enterprises was implemented at the start of 2008, ending the previous regime under which tax incentives had been offered to lure foreign investors to China. Partly because of this, the effective tax burden on FIEs is expected to rise in the medium term, but the initial impact is likely to be muted. There is a phase-in period during which existing benefits may still be enjoyed, and tax incentives will still be available (to both local firms and FIEs) for companies investing in targeted regions and economic sectors, such as high-tech industry and research and development. For some firms, however, the effect of the change could be serious.

Foreign companies should be aware of the impact of the tax changes on their Chinese competitors. This will vary from sector to sector, partly because many Chinese manufacturers have already routed their invest-ment via offshore locations so they can enjoy the same advantages as foreign investors. Some local governments may offer incentives in excess of those permitted under the new legislation to attract investors to districts under their control. Companies wishing to invest should be aware that if these incentives are later found to breach the law, the advantages gained may be clawed back by the tax authorities in subsequent years. China also switched from a production-based value-added tax system to a consumption-based one in 2009. This is expected to have less of an impact on foreign investors than the unification of the foreign and local tax rates, but it will eliminate double taxation and encourage fixed-asset investment, which will be taxed less heavily under the new system.

### Corporate income tax

Under the 2008 Corporate Income Tax Law (CIT law, also known as the Enterprise Income Tax law), foreign and domestic companies in China are subject to a unified income tax rate of 25% – though implementation could be uneven as changes are phased in and because of a number of exceptions.[3] These include foreign investors in technology or R&D and investments in regions officially encouraged by the central government (such as the western and northern regions of Tibet, Xinjiang and Inner Mongolia, which retain their ability to offer tax exemptions from the 40% of tax revenues that they retain). In a bid to remain attractive to foreign investors, local governments also increasingly offer non-tax incentives. For example, major cities such as Beijing, Shanghai and Guangzhou offer foreign investors various generous non-tax incentives ranging from one-off payments to rental subsidies, according to Titus Bongart, a Shanghai-based tax specialist and partner at global accounting firm Ernst & Young. Overall, however, the CIT law has weakened the profitability of foreign companies operating in China.

### Summary

- **Horses for courses.** While the WOFE is now the preferred investment vehicle for most foreign investors, joint ventures can offer some advantages.
- **Corporate tax: a level playing field.** The unification of the tax regime in 2008 brought to an end various forms of preferential tax treatment from which foreign investors had benefited for more than a decade. Some regions and investment zones are still able to offer limited incentives, but most multinationals are now subject to the same tax rates as local companies.

# 6 Making acquisitions work

The mightiest dragon cannot crush the local snake.
  From *Journey to the West*, a 16th-century Ming dynasty novel, published anonymously

Even before the global financial crisis multinational investors were pursuing the opportunities for growth offered by emerging markets, of which China is the biggest. Corporate investors generally favour acquisition as the means by which they can expand rapidly in these growth markets, and financial investors like to invest in dynamic companies seeking initial public offerings overseas. As regulatory changes in the financial markets improve, the environment governing foreign acquisitions in China is becoming more robust, prompting private equity investors to invest on a large scale as their exit strategies become more assured. This chapter reviews the industry and analyses the factors behind acquisitions in China that have succeeded or failed.

## The urge to merge: China's M&A environment

Mergers and acquisitions (M&A) have proved to be one of the preferred methods of investment in China for multinationals seeking to enter the mainland market or to expand existing operations. UK retailer Tesco, which came to China comparatively late in 2003, played catch-up by acquiring Hymall, a local retailer that already had a joint venture with Ting Hsin of Taiwan. In 2005–06, Italy's Luxottica acquired two mainland companies to become China's largest optician chain, with some 300 outlets.

M&A has had a short history in China. In 1985, when one of the first M&A was completed, transaction values totalled just $124m. Foreign investors generally preferred to enter the market through the joint-venture route, giving them little choice or flexibility. The opening up of the market following China's accession to the WTO in 2001, after 15 years of negotiations with the WTO and its previous incarnation GATT, helped to create a more liberal investment environment under which large-scale M&A could be accepted. At the same time, global M&A was booming and Chinese companies were (and remain) natural targets. M&A has continued to grow, promising to become a significant part of China's overall development. In 2009, M&A transactions totalled some $166 billion, according to Dealogic, a financial research firm. In a report jointly published by the Economist

Intelligence Unit and Mercer, a human resources company, 60% of 670 executives interviewed said that China, India and South-East Asia figured significantly in their companies' M&A strategies.

### Factors in M&A growth

- **WTO requirements.** The surge in M&A activity in China reflected the liberalisation of sectors where foreign investment was previously restricted. Most sectors due to be opened up to foreign investors have already completed the process, with just a small number remaining off-limits or heavily restricted.
- **Consolidation.** Many sectors and categories have traditionally been fragmented, with few players commanding more than 1–2% of national share. A shopper visiting a local hypermarket in a big city can choose from around 45 brands of shampoo or 20 brands of toothpaste. There are estimated to be more than 3,000 cosmetics brands in the Chinese market. The top five producers in the beer industry, for example, control just 40% of the market in China, and the top five brands just 14%. Compare those percentages with Japan (83% and 52%), South Korea (94% and 78%) and the United States (76% and 44%).
- **Capital influx.** China-focused private equity funds have helped drive M&A, and the regulatory environment governing M&A has evolved considerably since 2005 to create a more stable investment environment with exit possibilities for investors.
- **Rise of private companies.** The number and size of privately owned enterprises continue to grow, increasing the number of potential acquisition targets. The M&A process involving private enterprises is generally simpler than for SOEs, making them an even more attractive investment target.

Home-grown players have also used M&A in what can be a dog-eat-dog tussle. In the ferociously competitive consumer electronics sector, Gome and Suning have gobbled up most of their rivals in a bid to keep expanding and not be eaten themselves. Alibaba.com, in which Yahoo! owns a 39% stake, was planning to expand through the acquisition of smaller business-to-business websites in 2010, both at home and abroad. Meanwhile Lenovo, China's largest maker of personal computers by volume, was considering M&A opportunities in the BRIC countries, as well as organic growth. Lenovo acquired IBM's personal computer business in 2005.

The benefits of M&A are unquestionable. Investors can leapfrog years of organic growth, acquiring outlets, manufacturing plant, distribution networks, well-known brands, consumer markets and relationships (or *guanxi*). Unilever's acquisition of Laocai soy sauce in 1997 helped it expand its foods sector and localise its brand. M&A activity is the largest source of FDI in China, as it is elsewhere. Government moves towards consolidation are a leading driver in domestic M&A. Its aim for strategic industries such as commodities, telecoms and aviation is to build and nurture 5–10 national players through forced mergers and Darwinian legislation, ensuring that only the strongest survive. Ultimately, these national players will become international and, it is hoped, global players.

As it does elsewhere, M&A brings its own associated risks. Rigorous and effective due diligence is essential in China's opaque operating environment, particularly in areas such as shareholdings and shareholder reputation. A director at a US-based manufacturer found out too late about the links between his recently acquired joint-venture partner and the local city government, which resulted in troublesome efforts by the local authorities to intervene in operations when the joint venture started to become profitable.

Table 6.1 **Notable M&A deals in China, 2009**

| Rank | Partners | Status | Nature | Value ($bn) |
|------|----------|--------|--------|-------------|
| 1 | Chinalco-Rio Tinto | Failed | Outbound | 19.50 |
| 2 | Coca Cola-Huiyuan | Failed | Inbound | 2.30 |
| 3 | PetroChina & CNOOC-Repsol YPF | Ongoing | Outbound | 13.00–14.50 |
| 4 | Geely-Volvo | Done | Outbound | 2.00 |
| 5 | Tengzhong-Hummer | Done | Outbound | 100.00 |
| 6 | Yanzhou-Felix | Done | Outbound | 3.20 |
| 7 | China Eastern Airlines-Shanghai Airlines | Ongoing | Domestic | 1.20 |
| 8 | AVIC & ATL-FACC | Done | Outbound | 1.40 |
| 9 | Minmetals-Oz | Done | Outbound | 1.20 |
| 10 | Shanda-Hurray! | Done | Outbound | 0.05 |

Source: China.org.cn (www.china.org.cn/business/2009–12/28/content_19143161.htm)

### Regulating a growing market

As M&A has grown, so has the need to regulate and legislate. The nature of China's evolving regulatory environment and the arrival of a new invest-ment vehicle has led to some hard-fought turf wars between government bodies seeking to exert their authority over parts of the M&A process. In 2005–06, for example, the State Administration of Foreign Exchange (SAFE) issued three circulars detailing restrictions on foreign-invested M&A in China, only to have super-ministry Mofcom trump the SAFE circulars with its own regulations. Meanwhile, other industry-specific bodies such as the State Administration for Radio, Film and Television (SARFT) issued their own rules. Investors found that it was impossible to conduct the M&A process entirely legally because the regulations issued by different government entities contradicted each other. These contradic-tions have now largely been resolved.

Two principal rules affect foreign-invested M&A in China. They are The Provisional Rules on the Merger and Acquisition of Domestic Enterprises by Foreign Investors ("M&A Rules"), published in 2003 and updated in 2006, and the Anti-Monopoly Law ("AML"), published in 2007 and imple-mented in 2008.

### M&A Rules

Enacted in 2003 and updated in 2006 by a host of government acronyms (including Mofcom, SAIC, SAFE and SAT), the M&A Rules were a big step towards clearer regulation of foreign acquisitions in China and signalled government intentions to scrutinise inbound foreign M&A much more rigorously than in the past. The M&A Rules require Mofcom approval for any foreign acquisitions of local companies in key or sensitive areas or which threaten to take control of well-known trademarks or traditional brands. The M&A Rules cover two types of acquisition, equity-based and asset-based, where foreign investors buy either equity or assets within the target company.[1]

### The Anti-Monopoly Law

China's Anti-Monopoly Law (AML) came into effect in 2008 after a 13-year gestation period, and implementing regulations and clarifications followed in 2009. The passage of the law was a triumph if only because it demonstrated that there could be agreement between China's three anti-monopoly bodies: the NDRC, which is responsible for pricing; the SAIC, which assesses potential monopoly situations; and Mofcom, which covers overall M&A approvals. The AML started off smoothly in late

2008 with China's approval of an acquisition by Belgium-based InBev of US firm Anheuser-Busch with regard to the impact of the transaction on the Chinese beer sector (through Anheuser-Busch's stake in Tsingtao Brewery, which InBev subsequently sold to Japan's Asahi Breweries in 2009). However, controversy followed with Mofcom's rejection in 2009 of a \$2.4 billion bid by Coca-Cola the previous year for Huiyuan Juice Group, China's leading fruit-juice company, citing monopoly concerns. The proposed takeover was a politically sensitive deal which touched nationalist nerves and sparked public outrage that a foreign multinational company could acquire a home-grown brand – even though Huiyuan is now a Hong Kong-listed entity.

In late 2009 Mofcom ruled that Japanese firms Panasonic and Sanyo must sell off parts of their battery businesses in order to gain approval for their proposed merger. Some observers claimed the move was a protectionist one, but more importantly, it reflects China's growing status as a global antitrust authority on a par with the EU and Japan. The AML will take time to bed down. Foreign companies faced with potential AML action should work with the authorities, their own governments and chambers of commerce to ensure a clear understanding of the law and its application.

### Limiting M&A to help build globally competitive companies
In March 2009 the government announced plans to develop a "Big 10" group of globally competitive local automakers, led by Shanghai Automotive Industrial Corporation – partner to Volkswagen and General Motors. The plan was aimed at boosting sales and production to 10m units in 2009 and maintaining industry growth of around 10% for the next few years, according to the China Association of Automobile Manufacturers, an industry grouping. Foreign players such as General Motors, Volkswagen, Toyota and Hyundai will continue to hold minority stakes in local companies, but a goal of the plan is to raise the market share of domestic-brand cars from a 2009 level of 34% to more than 40%. Chinese monthly auto sales in 2008 climbed 6.7% to 9.38m units (the first time annual industry growth had fallen below 10% since 1999).

### Due diligence
An effective due diligence plan should cover the following.

### The due diligence team
A huge amount of information has to be processed and understood, and

investors often need dedicated resources to be able to handle these. To retain a sense of the acquisition senior management must be involved, so it is best not to outsource control of the due diligence process but just parts of it, such as financial due diligence to accountants. When the due diligence is completed, senior management should make a decision based on their "feel" for the deal. The due diligence team or local office of the acquiring company may not be able to make such a decision themselves because of the "deal fever" that may set in.

### Sources of information

The team should establish exactly what information is crucial to the decision-making process and what would be simply nice to know. Based on this, the team sets up an approach for the investigation, identifying all the sources to be used. At this stage, it helps to consider sources beyond the standard consultancies: workers and managers within the company; customers, distributors, suppliers, industry experts and specialist consulting firms outside the company.

### General checklist

Each acquisition requires its own specific checklist. A partner at one of the Big Four accounting firms based in Shanghai is dismissive of the increasing vogue for "online data rooms", a type of financial due diligence where much of the auditing is conducted remotely rather than sitting in data rooms in the target company's office. He estimates that his team gathers some two-thirds of the quality information it needs by spending time on the target company's premises talking to staff, workers and management informally. The quality of the information is always more important than the quantity. Checklists typically include:

- strategy and background;
- markets, products and marketing;
- distribution and sales;
- financial audit;
- manufacturing and technology;
- environmental audit;
- legal audit;
- organisation structure and human resources.

### Reputation

Due diligence will help give you a more informed understanding of a company's legal standing and financial health, but it is often difficult to get a true feel for your target. Spending time with the principals – the owners, senior management and others – and researching their backgrounds will provide a clearer understanding of the personality, business style, reputation and professional track record of the principal players in the deal. Critical factors or "red flags" to look out for include:

- unclear source of capital;
- opaque ownership structures;
- poor regulatory track record;
- weak internal controls with regard to corporate governance/ business ethics;
- dependency on political relationships;
- possible criminal links.

Reputational due diligence also serves to flag up issues that could be used to seek a better price for the acquisition. These can range from direct or indirect ownership (through relatives) of small entities affiliated to the target company to long-standing relationships with local government officials (whose ability to interfere with the business or political behaviour may be called into question further down the line).

### Mind your IP
Foreign investors involved in M&A remain understandably wary about transferring sensitive intellectual property, especially in the technology sphere (see Chapter 4).

### Build consensus
As investors build consensus among the interested parties, they should plan for what they would like to happen and when. This should involve not only laying off unnecessary employees but also changing the venture's organisational structure to make it function better. As when starting from scratch, the foreign investor should examine the business by department to work out how many staff are needed and who should fill those slots. Any new human resources policies or incentive systems designed to help the venture function better should also be introduced.

### Going in with eyes open

A private equity firm carried out due diligence into the reputation of an acquisition target, a local chemicals company, in northern China, having already conducted financial, legal and environment due diligence work on the company. Public-record checks confirmed that there were no issues relating to the shareholder structure and ownership history of the company, but the absence of financial data covering the period when the target company moved from state ownership to private ownership raised a potential red flag, which was noted. This area was subsequently checked by the audit consultant and was resolved.

The private equity firm then commissioned reputational checks on the acquisition target. These showed that the target company was perceived by the local community to be a major polluter, despite the positive results of the environmental due diligence. It transpired that the acquisition target's "clean technology" was used only occasionally and that the company routinely dumped effluent in the local water supply. The acquisition did not go through.

### *Dairy consolidation: streamlining isn't always enough*

The government uses an enforced M&A policy to consolidate and stream-line industries where there are too many players and the sector itself is suffering for whatever reason (often substandard products or services). After the dairy industry suffered widespread losses in 2007 and was hit by a scandal involving baby-milk powder tainted with a chemical, melamine,[2] in 2008, consolidation and increased competition were seen as the best way to resolve quality issues and streamline the sector to make regulatory enforcement and monitoring easier. The top five dairy processors control some 40% of the market, with the remainder split between 700 smaller firms that have carved out market share in particular regions or categories.

The NDRC has encouraged industry players to expand production through M&A and asset restructuring. The dairy sector has come under even greater pressure than other fragmented industries – such as steel and automotive – to consolidate because streamlining sectors reduces the number of players, making regulation and monitoring easier. Ultimately, the government hopes to produce sector champions with nationwide operations and sufficient structure to become global players.

## Summary

- **China is a patchwork of fragmented markets.** Don't be seduced by the thought of selling a pair of widgets to every Chinese consumer.
- **Time is precious.** Allow sufficient time and resources to carry out thorough due diligence at every level.
- **Do your due diligence.** Use due diligence to identify a target's weaknesses and make use of these during the negotiation process. Ask yourself: Is the target really as attractive as it appears to outsiders? Will the target fit into our overall sales and growth plans? Can we restructure and manage the target in a way that will bring profitable growth to the business?
- **Look for "red flags".** Certain telltale signs will alert you to potential problems in the future.
- **Beware of the data.** Treat all numbers with extreme caution.
- **Get close up and personal.** To get a feel for the target and the deal, have due diligence team members on the ground and close to the process.
- **Where's the money?** Focus on real future earnings potential.

# 7 Human resources: attracting and retaining talent

Make happy those who are near, and those who are far will come.

Confucian Analects Book XIII

As multinational investors devolve greater responsibility to country-based managers, demand for mid-level talent has surged. Attracting and especially retaining talented staff is becoming a growing problem for employers, making appealing job packages and employee development essential.

## China's labour market

China's human resources are abundant. The problem is finding the right people for your operation. The supply of unskilled labour remains as vast as ever, but the shortage of skilled labour in the major cities has grown increasingly acute over the past decade. At the same time unemployment, a perennial problem, increased markedly in late 2008 and early 2009 as the global economic crisis hit export-processing companies. Only around 30% of the 23m migrant workers who returned to their home villages for their annual Chinese New Year holiday in February 2009 went back to their jobs in coastal cities after the break.

In addition, some 4–6m college and university graduates enter the job pool each year. Yet unemployment among well-educated people is also rising for various reasons. Chief among these are the dispersed nature of graduates, who may be unwilling or unable to move because of *hukou* restrictions (see page 135) or family ties (caring for elderly parents or relatives), and the return of overseas graduates, adding to the supply.

The shortage of skilled labour is acute in certain sectors: senior management, sales promotion, machinery repair, textile manufacturing and a host of other specific skill sets in key industries. As salaries have risen and competition has grown, companies in Guangdong have experienced acute labour shortages in manufacturing and assembly operations. Makers of semiconductors, cleantech[1] and cell phones, and companies researching biotech and stem cell research have all had difficulties finding and retaining local talent. Many new jobs require a high level of education and expertise not possessed by jobless state workers.

Where Chinese people work has changed dramatically. A shift towards urbanisation and increasing worker migration has lowered the proportion of China's labour force employed in rural areas from roughly three-quarters in 1990 to less than two-thirds as of 2009. By 2030, the government hopes the rural proportion will fall further to one-third as urbanisation continues and the employment structure shifts from primary to tertiary industry. In both urban and rural areas, the proportion of people working in the state sector has fallen sharply as SOEs have been closed down, while workforces at the growing number of private and foreign-invested enterprises continue to grow. In the cities, private companies now offer almost as many employment opportunities as SOEs.

The story for foreign investors is a frustrating one. Over the next five years, foreign-invested enterprises (FIEs), including joint ventures, will need to employ some 3m local workers, around 1m of whom will be college graduates. Yet of the 4m students graduating from college each year, only about 1.2m are "suitable" for FIEs, according to a report published by McKinsey & Co; just 10% (400,000) have sufficient work experience and English-language capabilities to work for FIEs in areas such as engineering, finance, accounting, quantitative analysis, life-science research, medicine, nursing and office support. Naturally, there is significant competition for these high-end college graduates, since Chinese companies are also keen to grab quality staff.

**A growing, greying burden for China's generation of single children**

32  average age in China
45  predicted average age in 2050
7.9  number of working-age people for each person in China above the age of 65
2.35  predicted number of working-age people per each 65+ Chinese in 2050.

A worrying trend for China's urban unemployment is the growing proportion of new graduates without jobs joining the ranks of poorly educated or middle-aged workers. Part of the problem is that since the early 2000s universities and colleges have been producing more graduates in an effort to meet demand for a more highly educated labour force. Yet university curricula have not prepared students adequately for finding work in the rapidly evolving job market, and specialist institutes that would have provided more practical skills have not received the government funding they need. The government may respond by limiting the higher-education intake and beefing up high-school diplomas, or providing much-needed support for vocational colleges.

## Professional staff

### Expatriates

Expatriate workers are people who do not have Chinese citizenship. They are typically brought in from the head office of multinational companies or are hired locally from other foreign firms in China to fill senior management or strategically critical positions. Expatriates on a full package from Europe or North America are usually expensive, though those hired locally are not. Both are subject to the same labour laws.

Multinationals' attitudes to localisation – the replacement of expatriate staff with local hires – can best be described as cyclical. In the 1990s, in a bid to cut costs, many companies "localised" senior management, replacing western expatriates with overseas Chinese (from Hong Kong, Malaysia, Taiwan and Singapore as well as from Australia, Canada, the UK and the United States) and occasionally mainland Chinese, though initially this led to problems with strategy and decision-making. For many companies the combination of local business knowledge and an international perspective has proved immensely successful – Yum! Foods in China is controlled by senior Taiwanese management – even if it has worked out just as expensive as using non-Chinese expatriates in most cases. Asian expatriates, especially from Taiwan and Singapore, are believed to account for over half of all expatriates recruited for positions in China. Returnees, in particular, have taken most of the senior positions offered. As one British advertising executive says, "It's the common sense that makes the difference."

Localisation (which can also refer to transferring expatriate staff on to local pay and/or benefits similar to local staff) is one of the tougher problems senior management face in China. As well as finding competent candidates with the experience and skills required, foreign investors have to invest time in training candidates for management roles to the point where they fully understand the business, have the full respect of all staff (no mean achievement in offices which typically contain local nationals from many different parts of the country) and can represent the business effectively in the professional arena.

At present, both foreign and domestic companies have difficulty

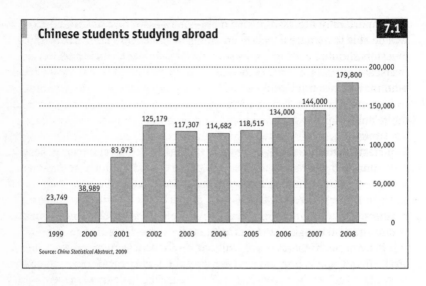

**Chinese students studying abroad** `7.1`

Source: *China Statistical Abstract*, 2009

finding local staff qualified to take over top positions, such as country manager and senior management. The shortage of suitably qualified staff has held back many multinational companies in China. This is largely because most local staff have not had sufficient time to develop modern management skills and experience in leadership, decision-making and risk-taking. MBA programmes have been particularly successful in China because they are supposed to help develop these skills, as well as honing strategic and analytical capabilities. One European CEO still hires expatriates "for international insights into attitude and culture" and "to excite the young work force who want to be international without being able to leave home".

### Overseas returnees

Multinational employers looking for Chinese staff with overseas experience or an international outlook often turn to "returnees" – Chinese nationals who have studied or worked abroad and subsequently return to China. Between 1985 and 2005, 679,000 students went abroad to study, many of them graduates of China's leading universities. Of these, roughly 25% eventually returned, though that percentage is believed to have risen with China's economic boom and the global financial crisis.

Since around 2001, growing numbers of overseas returnees have provided an important combination of skilled professionals, spanning the divide between international expertise and local business culture – though it is important not to assume that a Shanghainese returnee, for example, will be able to manage a local team in Beijing effectively. Similarly, foreign investors should be aware of the sometimes sensitive dynamics between overseas returnees, outwardly confident and worldly wise, and local staff, who may be resentful (and not a little envious) of a newcomer claiming to be "one of them". This tension is not new, having long been part of the relationship between mainland and overseas Chinese. In the 1990s the Hong Kong-based Chinese finance director at a European consulting firm created considerable friction in the company's representative offices in Beijing and Shanghai because mainland staff found his somewhat brusque Cantonese manner to be arrogant and condescending.

Nevertheless, the experience and skills learnt at leading colleges, business schools and corporations in the United States, Canada, Europe and Australia can make returnees invaluable for multinational companies seeking international-standard skills at middle or senior management level. However, it is important to manage salary and career expectations carefully.

### Returnees in the state sector: from turtles to seaweed

Over the past decade the number of Chinese students returning from education overseas has grown markedly. These graduates, known in Chinese as *haigui* (sea turtles), are perceived to have greater business acumen, training and international experience, and consequently are sought after by local governments for management or technical positions in centrally approved new ventures at industrial and high-tech parks across the country. Perks can include relatively higher pay, tax incentives, preferential housing, children's schooling and employment for spouses. Returnees who accept such posts are also allowed to keep their long-term or permanent residence in foreign countries.

Sadly, the sheer number of *haigui* and the perhaps unrealistic expectations on the part of both the authorities and the returnees themselves has tarnished their reputation. They are now more commonly referred to in Shanghai as *haidai* (seaweed, which in Mandarin sounds similar to "waiting for a job"). Returnees appear better suited to private enterprise than the state sector.

### College graduates: grow your own talent
Multinational companies often find that it is cost-effective to employ

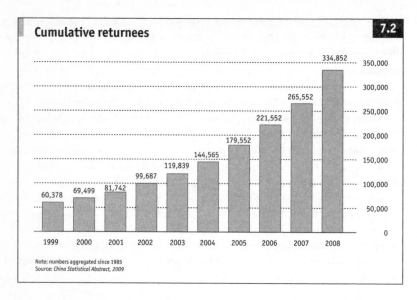

**Cumulative returnees** 7.2

Note: numbers aggregated since 1985
Source: *China Statistical Abstract, 2009*

graduates straight out of college and train them on the job. This "grow-your-own" option enables employers to pay low salaries and spot up-and-coming junior professionals with the potential to become senior managers in 5–7 years' time. For graduates, the opportunity to work in an FIE brings huge opportunities in terms of career development and experience, and competition for entry-level management jobs with foreign companies is fierce.

The government has also sought to raise the English-language skills of new graduates, with English being taught from secondary-school level. It has also employed more foreign teachers and has opened up its education and training markets to foreign investment. In September 2008, Guangdong's local government announced plans to build 12 vocational high schools in the Pearl River Delta over the next few years. These will train 100,000 students a year from less-developed areas of Guangdong to meet soaring demand for skilled workers in the region. The schools, each with 5,000–10,000 students, will help the delta region grapple with a long-standing labour shortage. At the same time, there is a surplus of unskilled workers in the province's north, east and west. An education official said that by 2011 the province aimed to train 2m students a year, up from 1.3m in 2007. Also in September 2008, Jinan in Shandong province began providing free career training to unemployed university graduates who could not find jobs a year after graduating.

## Know your human resources terminology

### Dang'an

Employee's personal file. Every Chinese citizen is assigned an identification number at birth, and the authorities create a file that will track that person's life history: residence, education, employment, family history, religious affiliation, political and criminal records. When a person moves city or transfers jobs, the *dang'an* must also be transferred.

### Hukou

Citizen's household registration or residence permit. Every Chinese citizen has a *hukou*, which provides details of his or her place of birth and details of family relatives. Introduced at the start of the PRC in 1949, the *hukou* system helped the authorities organise and control supplies of daily essentials – and ultimately all social welfare benefits such as housing and schooling – to urban populations. The *hukou* system seems an anachronism in today's market economy, but it is still used to track population movement and growth. Importantly, employees arriving in new cities must try to transfer their *hukou* to the new location as soon as possible so that they may enrol their children in school and enjoy state health care. It can be a difficult process because of the unprecedented mobility of the working population and the state's reticence in transferring a *hukou* for any reason other than a permanent move. This is why most of the country's 140m or so rural migrants effectively exist as a subclass in cities, attending migrant schools and health clinics outside the mainstream institutions.

Foreign investors will come face-to-face with the *hukou* issue when local employees or candidates are forced to refuse albeit attractive relocations or lucrative new positions because they cannot move their *hukou* and so would lose all social welfare benefits were they to accept the positions. The *hukou* system is being relaxed and reformed but this will take time.

### Danwei

Work unit. This is less important than it used to be. Until 1979 the *danwei* provided jobs and associated social welfare benefits in the form of the "iron rice bowl". The most important political group at the local level, the *danwei* held *dang'ans* and other information about its employees. Now local labour bureaus generally hold such details, and the *danwei* is only of any importance in rural areas.

### Xiagang

Broadly equivalent to "outplacement", *xiagang* refers to the practice among state-owned enterprises of telling workers not to report for work and paying them a nominal monthly wage and social benefits. The *xiagang* system softened the impact of SOE reforms in the early 2000s by providing basic support for the millions of laid-off workers for whom new employment could not be found. The scheme continues today.

## The migrant workforce

The first farmers to leave the countryside in search of work in the big cities arrived in Shenzhen in the mid-1980s, lured by rapid urban development. As the economic boom spread northwards from the special economic zones in Guangdong to Shanghai, Beijing and the north-east, the exodus of rural migrants became a flood, culminating in the largest movement of people in history. Two decades later, an estimated 150m migrant workers – nearly half of them under 25 – were providing cheap labour for factories, construction sites and infrastructure projects all down the east coast. Yet by 2004, labour-intensive industries (such as textiles, shoes and mobile-phone manufacturing) in Guangdong were starting to report shortages of skilled labour – in a province where a quarter of all workers are migrants and where nearly one-third of the country's migrant workers are based. The labour shortage grew increasingly acute as manufacturers sought to cut costs while struggling to produce higher-quality goods.

There are two main reasons for the labour shortage. First, the cost of living in coastal provinces has increased markedly; in most cases, more than the migrant worker wages that cost-cutting manufacturers are prepared to pay. Second, as the lot of farmers has gradually improved – in part because of the abolition of farm tax and other levies – they have become less willing to leave their homes and travel thousands of miles to unfamiliar, unfriendly cities in search of work.

The challenge for the government is enormous. Not only have rural migrant workers provided an invaluable source of income to under-nourished parts of the rural economy through their remittances, thereby feeding at least a little of the coastal wealth into needy inland regions; they have also provided a crucial labour-cost advantage that has helped fuel economic growth, whether it be in urban construction projects or low value-add manufacturing or export-processing plants in the south and east. Now the government must find ways to reabsorb tens of millions of young workers (mainly male, mainly single) into the rural economy without exacerbating dangerous social tensions.

Another factor is the emergence of second-generation migrant workers – the children of the migrants who led the initial movement to the cities in the late 1980s and early 1990s. Second-generation migrant workers generally resemble permanent city residents in terms of behaviour, appearance and even education – most of them having received a secondary education – rather than their parents. They also differ from their parents in being happy to work for more than a single employer, having higher salary expectations and being intolerant of physically demanding work in poor conditions.

## Recruitment

Once a virtual lottery controlled by state-run labour bureaus, China's recruitment market has matured and diversified to offer most of the recruiting channels that employers would find in the West. Familiar sources such as headhunters, direct advertising, job fairs, online recruiting and campus recruitment are supplemented by the more Chinese practice of relying on labour-service corporations and joint-venture partners.

- **Headhunters.** Most major international executive search firms (or headhunters) have representative offices in China, and there are believed to be over 4,000 local recruiting firms. Headhunters operate in China as they would in the United States or Europe, developing networks in particular sectors to locate suitable candidates for positions that become available. Usually this means poaching an executive from one company to be hired by a rival firm. Search firms often specialise by industry. Wholly foreign-owned headhunting firms are still forbidden.
- **Direct advertising.** Advertising in Chinese newspapers is surprisingly expensive and rarely reaches the kind of specialised, technical or experienced employees sought by foreign companies. Trade and industry magazines reach a more targeted audience and as a result offer a better option.
- **Job fairs.** The job fair concept is still hugely popular in China, and thousands take place each year in schools and exhibition centres in major cities across the country. As with newspaper advertising, job fairs appeal to a broad audience, making the selection of suitable candidates a time-consuming process. The sheer number of job fairs also makes it difficult for foreign companies to decide which ones to attend. It is worth contacting the organisers to find out which other multinationals will be present at the events that are of interest.
- **Online recruitment.** Online recruitment has surged in popularity as internet use has grown (by March 2010, China had 400m internet users). Specialisation

is possible and this platform helps narrow the list of potential candidates, but a face-to-face meeting remains essential. Foreign companies should bear in mind that recruitment websites may be out of date as some are updated only sporadically.

- **Campus recruitment.** In recruiting from campuses, multinational companies have gone to the source for management-calibre talent, even if candidates have no practical experience. The Big Four accounting firms, some of the first foreign players to exploit this channel, typically recruit hundreds of graduates from campuses each year. Students are motivated and smart, having been through China's tough university admissions process. They are also keen to learn, having valuable technical knowledge but no experience. Recruitment cycles typically start at the beginning of the academic year in October and are finalised around Chinese New Year in the spring.
- **Labour-service corporations.** In the 1980s the government created a number of labour-service corporations to manage the flow of Chinese employees to foreign companies and representative offices. Nowadays foreign companies, joint ventures and local companies may hire employees themselves, but representative offices are still required officially to hire their staff through labour-service corporations; and because they handle many of the employee welfare programmes – benefits, legal consulting, transfers of *hukou* and *dang'an* – foreign companies often find it more convenient to outsource recruitment. The first and most well-known labour-service corporation is the Foreign Enterprise Service Corp (FESCO) in Beijing, which also has offices in Tianjin, Shanghai, Guangzhou and Shenzhen. The role of these corporations may change significantly with the impending passage of the Labour Contract Law.
- **Hiring from a local partner.** Multinationals should be wary of hiring staff from their local joint-venture partner or acquisition target. Some staff are doubtless essential to the smooth operation of the business, but local partners have a tendency to offload many less important employees. This is particularly the case when SOEs are involved. Foreign companies have frequently been asked to take on the cost of excess staff who are still on the company books but who receive a basic wage for staying at home as part of China's *xiagang* (outplacement) system. To prevent this happening, foreign investors need a say in – or ideally control over – the hiring and firing process during the negotiations and after the transaction is completed.

Senior local managers are highly sought-after. Foreign and local companies alike resort to poaching high-quality managers from rival firms by offering substantially higher salaries, regardless of the likelihood that these individuals will move on in similar fashion in as little as 18 months. Many employers offer financial incentives for staff that refer candidates who are successfully hired. As with all hires, due diligence – even a basic background screening – is essential.

### Employee turnover

Staff turnover at FIEs in China is thought to be as much as twice the global average. Employee retention is particularly tough in big cities where talented local managers with 5–10 years' experience of working in an FIE are sought after by multinationals entering the market or expanding their operations. In China's generally underpaid market, local managers may move from company to company for a salary increase of just a few hundred dollars. Job-hopping is most frequent among young staff, skilled migrant workers and – most frustratingly – senior managers. High churn rates drive up labour costs and can be disruptive to business.

#### *Managing and retaining local staff*

Senior managers in China generally spend more time managing and developing local staff than their counterparts in the West. For local employees, senior managers are expected to provide guidance, direction and effective communication, and to show an interest in the personal lives and longer-term professional development of individual staff. Local workforces respond enthusiastically and positively to social activities outside the workplace; these help to develop stronger personal connections with management and so foster a positive working environment.

Many multinational companies run programmes and other initiatives to develop staff. These include seconding managers to different business units to deepen management experience, introducing cross-functional projects to help local staff in their professional development, setting up mentoring programmes and running leadership training modules. One international accounting firm regularly sends promising staff to overseas offices for periods ranging from eight months to two years.

Such methods help not only to create more rounded and valued staff, but also to raise retention levels in a market notorious for job-hopping and starved of local professionals with industry experience. Employees who are challenged by their work and feel appreciated in their roles will be less likely to accept offers from would-be employers.

#### *Training*

Training is fundamental to developing management skills and also to staff retention. The human resources director at a US manufacturing company with operations across China says she values training as much as a tool for retaining valued managers as for the greater skills it provides. Training can range from evening classes in English or Microsoft Excel to mentoring or short-term secondments to MBA programmes (see below). Local (private and state-owned) and foreign companies alike budget for training, spending as much as 15% of annual salaries in the case of private or foreign-invested operations.

## The MBAs of China

Multinational companies value MBAs because these qualifications are perceived to confer an international outlook on local candidates. Proficiency in English is increasingly a necessity for applications to multinational companies, though practical work experience and an ability to think and work independently often count for more.

In 1991, China's Ministry of Education (MOE) approved only nine MBA programmes but by 2005, 89 institutions were running more than 160 MBA programmes throughout China, including Hong Kong. Even so, only around 3,000 students graduate with MBAs each year. Part of the problem is that only one student in seven passes the entrance exam. An additional factor is the falling growth rate of MBA graduate salaries. MBA course materials in China almost mirror those of North American business schools, which have sought to tap into the booming Chinese market by establishing joint MBA programmes and – in some cases – colleges and campuses.

However, it is the Executive MBA (EMBA) programme which has proved most popular in China, with senior management – chief executives, directors, chairmen and company presidents – making up the majority of EMBA students. All are seeking to learn western management practices that they can then introduce to their companies, no matter whether they are private or state-owned.

The China-Europe International Business School (CEIBS) was founded in 1994. In the school's short history, its MBA programme has become a leader in the Asia-Pacific region, reaching 8th place in the *Financial Times* global rankings in 2009, making it the first Chinese business school to make the top ten. CEIBS's MBA programme has been ranked top in Asia for six consecutive years (2004–09). Its EMBA programme came 26th in 2009 (and 4th in China and Hong Kong), according to the *Financial Times* global MBA rankings.

The top five EMBA programmes in China and Hong Kong (with global rankings in parentheses) in 2009, according to the *Financial Times*, were:

1   Kellogg/Hong Kong UST School of Business and Management (1st)
2   Washington University in St Louis/Olin School of Business (12th)
3   Chinese University of Hong Kong (19th)
4   China-Europe International Business School (26th)
5   OneMBA: CUHK/RSM/UNC/FGV São Paulo/EGADE (27th)

### Cultural differences

Foreign bosses who manage local staff highlight six cultural aspects that require special attention:

- **Initiative.** In a culture where individual decisions and actions are tacitly discouraged, it can be difficult to find staff who are happy to take decisions and accept responsibility for the consequences. Individualism can be perceived to be non-conformist – a negative trait in China's homogeneous society – and local management rarely exhibit or encourage it when communicating with local employees.
- **Harmony.** Local staff feel uncomfortable with conflict or hostility. Charged environments inevitably affect staff morale and productivity.
- **Status and self-respect.** Local staff are mortified by the notion of a dressing-down in front of colleagues. To preserve "face" or self-respect, critical comments and frank appraisals should be carefully prepared and made one-on-one behind closed doors.
- **Communication.** Bosses should communicate clearly to local staff, but it is also important to encourage upward communication. Traditional notions of hierarchy inhibit this behaviour in a society where authority is rarely questioned.
- **Ethics.** Chinese partners and employees are open to considering ethical issues but will resist what they see as western paternalism if foreign ethical models are imposed on local situations. Foreign executives in China should start by acknowledging the ethical shortcomings of many countries. They should also encourage local managers to revise existing codes of conduct or even create their own ethical codes to generate greater ownership of them.
- **Nationalism.** Foreign bosses should be extremely sensitive towards any perceived criticism of China, its history, culture and policies. Public indignation at China's former exploitation by

colonial powers runs through society at all levels, classes and generations, cutting through any loyalties towards corporate commitments (or friendships with foreigners). Discussion of sensitive political issues (Tibet and Taiwan, for example) and international diplomatic incidents (US-Chinese spats in international airspace or international waters) should be avoided.

### The M&A angle

One of the most important challenges facing the management team of a merger or acquisition is how best to handle the human resources aspects of the transition. Typically, a special HR team is created to handle the principal tasks, which include:

- identifying the strengths of the combined workforce – which can be highlighted to demonstrate the benefits of the merger or acquisition;
- assessing the quality of the new workforce and how much training and development will be required;
- assessing which staff and teams to retain and which to terminate;
- estimating payroll and benefit budgets and liabilities for the post-merger workforce;
- addressing potential cultural problems through the creation of cross-cultural teams, which organise social events based on team-building and orientation;
- creating new employee handbooks, codes of conduct and other company manuals;
- communicating clear messages to key staff throughout the transition period via meetings, briefings, intranet and literature.

## The Labour Contract Law

The Labour Contract Law (also known as the Employment Contract Law) was introduced in 2008 with the chief aim of strengthening the rights of hundreds of millions of workers – notably the estimated 140m migrant workers who have endured poor working conditions and abuse at the hands of their employers, particularly in the southern provinces. The law provides greater protection for workers from unfair dismissal in the event of mass lay-offs. It also requires employers to inform local governments of any lay-off involving more than 20 employees or 10% of the workforce. But it did not stop the surge in lay-offs in late 2008 and early 2009 that followed the onset of the global financial crisis.

The law also:

- prohibits the repeated use of short-term contracts that enabled employers to pay minimum benefits and jettison workers without having to state a cause for dismissal;
- encourages greater union representation and requires consultations with trade unions for the termination of employees;
- stipulates longer probation periods for new employees;
- restricts employers' use of "non-compete" clauses for staff leavers.

Overall, the law undeniably improves working conditions for employees, but foreign investors should be aware of the increasing employment costs that accompany it, along with rising average salaries, which were expected to climb by more than 6% in 2009.[2]

## Summary

- **Take me to your decision-maker.** Finding independent-minded local managers can be hard.
- **Share the love.** Motivate and retain local talent with more than just salaries.
- **Who are we hiring?** Screen all staff, no matter how junior.

# 8 Dealing with corruption and financial crime

Corruption is authority plus monopoly minus transparency.

Anon

Kill a chicken to frighten the monkey.

Chinese proverb often attributed to Mao Zedong

China, like other emerging markets, suffers from official corruption and financial crime. What makes it different is the scale of the bureaucracy and the pace of economic development from a low base, both of which have created conditions ideally suited to the growth of corruption and opportunities for massive financial gain by underpaid local government officials. This chapter looks at the seriousness of the issues facing China, the efforts the government is making in this area, and the measures multinational companies can take to minimise the risk to their Chinese operations.

## Official corruption: a perennial problem

China's authorities define corruption as the "abuse of public power (*gonggong quanli*) by occupants of public office (*gongzhi renyuan*) in the state and party apparatus for private interests".[1] Transparency International, an anti-corruption organisation, has a similar definition: "the abuse of public power for private gain". Corruption (*fubai* in Chinese, literally meaning "decay and putrefaction") is historically a part of daily life and can be traced back thousands of years. Endemic corruption in the later centuries of the Zhou dynasty (1045–256BC) is believed to have helped Confucius – who experienced graft and corruption at first hand while serving as a government official – seek to re-establish the ancient traditions of honour, morality and social hierarchies which he believed would check the empire's decline.

More than 2,000 years later, peasants in impoverished Guizhou province launched protests in 1851 amid famines and local government corruption as the Qing dynasty (1644–1911) drew to a close. By this time, the sheer volume of knowledge required to succeed in the Imperial examinations elevated cheating to something of an art form in China. Shirts had Confucian texts in tiny lettering sewn inside their cuffs; fans were designed with notes inscribed on their hidden side; even miniature books were made so that they could be concealed in the palm of the hand. Some candidates resorted to hiring experienced scholars to sit exams in their place; others simply bribed examiners.

Mao's Communist Party of China (CPC) rode to power in 1949 on the back of long-running anti-corruption campaigns against Chiang Kai-shek's ruling Kuomintang (Chinese Nationalist Party). Yet the CPC's dominant position, combined with economic hardship, meant that poorly paid party officials continued to use their positions for personal gain. A decade after China reopened its doors to foreign investment, official corruption re-emerged as a principal source of frustration, fuelling the Tian'anmen Square protests of 1989. Despite the continual anti-corruption campaigns and increasingly stringent penalties that followed, corruption has not gone away. China ranked 72nd out of 180 nations profiled in the 2009 Corruption Perceptions Index published by Transparency International (with the most corrupt countries ranking most highly).[2]

In a clear correlation with market reform, corruption has grown over the past three decades, relying on the presence of two factors: opportunity, presented to officials in the form of "the extensive role of government as a regulator, allocator, producer and employer", according to Sun Yan, author of *Corruption and Market in Contemporary China*;[3] and motivation, such as "confusion over changing values; weakness of moral sanctions; relative impoverishment; and a lack of alternative access to self-enrichment". That rapid economic development has benefited private entrepreneurs far more than it has government officials has been an additional source of aggravation, and the privatisation of state assets has put numerous opportunities for official graft within tempting reach of poorly paid bureaucrats.

At the same time, central government has decentralised much of the decision-making process for investment, as well as law enforcement. Many officials still feel that the government's message – "to get rich is glorious" – applies to them too. Hidden costs present considerable challenges, often appearing in the form of "fees". A businessman working with a joint venture in central China in the 1990s lists some of these unofficial levies: birth control fee, public health fee, public security fee, traffic control fee, tree-planting fee, fire department fee. High-level, high-stakes corruption increased to a greater extent than other forms of official corruption in the 1990s, according to Andrew Wedeman, a professor specialising in China at the University of Nebraska-Lincoln in the United States. This has remained the case since 2000.

## Consequences for society

Endemic corruption has numerous consequences for society, not least product scandals, which can stir up public anger. In 2008, a scandal over tainted baby-milk powder shook the public's faith in the government's ability to protect its consumers. Around 20 dairy producers had produced baby-milk powder containing melamine, a toxic chemical used in plastic production, which appears to boost the protein level in foods. At least six babies died and nearly 300,000 became ill, sparking public outrage and prompting the government to try to clean up the industry and introduce tougher food safety regulations. Despite these efforts, scandals in this industry re-emerged in 2009.

Public anger over corruption also erupted after a massive earthquake in south-western Sichuan in 2008 killed nearly 90,000 people and destroyed 80% of the buildings at its epicentre in Beichuan county. The earthquake, second only in modern Chinese history to the Tangshan earthquake that left 240,000 dead in 1976, highlighted the poor quality of numerous school buildings which collapsed while other buildings were left standing. Local media claimed that corruption and embezzlement had led to substandard construction. Nor did it stop there. In 2010 China's National Audit Office (NAO) reported that Rmb230m ($33.7m) of funds earmarked for reconstruction in the region had been misused. A number of party officials were subsequently punished.

## Bribery in high places

The most dramatic corruption case in modern Chinese history resulted in the arrest in 2006 of Chen Liangyu, Shanghai party secretary, in a scandal involving misappropriation and misallocation of some $450m in public pension funds. In 2008, Chen received an 18-year jail sentence for bribery and abuse of power in the first of a series of five cases of official corruption at the highest level. A major bribery case in the notoriously corrupt pharmaceutical sector led to the execution of the head of the State Food and Drug Administration (SFDA). Liu Zhihua, a former vice-mayor of Beijing and chief director of the agency supervising construction projects, including the city's $43 billion preparations for the 2008 Olympic Games, received a suspended death sentence for receiving some $1m in bribes between 1999 and 2006. Liu's lavish lifestyle involved big spending on villas, holidays and mistresses – all covered in salacious detail by China's increasingly inquisitive print media.

These and other cases doubtless prompted the authorities to draft a law giving them power to jail family members and mistresses of corrupt officials for more than seven years if they are found guilty of having taken advantage of the official's position to receive bribes or make money in other illegal ways. In 2009 Interpol sought to locate a relative of Macau's chief executive for allegedly providing kickbacks to the former public works minister jailed for 27 years in 2008 on 57 counts of bribe-taking, money-laundering, abuse of power and so on. The State Environmental Protection Agency (SEPA – China's environmental watchdog) also suffered a high-level bribery scandal, while the government ran high-profile trials of local officials found guilty of bribery and abuse of power in Fujian province in 2009 and Chongqing municipality in 2010.

In the first 11 months of 2009, some 107,000 officials were punished or disciplined and a total of Rmb4.4 billion ($647m) in public funds recovered, according to the Ministry of Supervision.

### Anti-corruption plan

The outbreak of high-level corruption scandals prompted the CPC's Central Committee to launch a five-year anti-corruption plan focusing on preventative measures, such as educating and supervising officials and improving the country's judicial system. In 2009, Gansu Provincial Corruption Prevention Bureau, the first provincial body of its kind, opened in Lanzhou, capital of Gansu province. The backdrop for these tougher actions is the leadership's concern that official corruption is eating away at the CPC's legitimacy and standing in the eyes of the public. An online survey carried out by www.people.com.cn, a local news portal, in the run-up to the annual session of the NPC in 2010 placed corruption at the top of the list for government action. In a survey of nearly 50,000 people carried out by Xinhua before the annual session of the NPC in 2009, over 75% named corruption as the most important issue facing the government. A similar survey carried out by Sina.com, a local internet portal, also cited corruption as the top concern, as did a survey of urban and rural residents' life satisfaction published the previous year by the Chinese Academy of Social Sciences (CASS) in its 2008 Blue Paper of Society.

These concerns were effectively highlighted in 2007, when a government website set up by the newly formed National Bureau of Corruption Prevention (NBCP) crashed hours after its launch as hundreds of thousands of visitors sought to register their complaints. The creation of the NBCP is in line with requirements set by the United Nations Convention Against Corruption (UNCAC). The Chinese government has also published a Five-Year Plan (2008–12) for Building and Completing the

System for Punishing and Preventing Corruption, and has tabled the Anti-Money Laundering Law and the Regulations on Disclosure of Government Information.

The CPC knows that its continuing grip on power depends largely on its ability to keep a lid on corruption and graft. The government punished more than 90,000 officials in 2006, and a national audit for that year discovered misuse of Rmb46.9 billion ($6.9 billion) in government funds – albeit a 53% reduction on 2005. In 2008, the CPC warned officials to guard against the "ten taboos". These include offering bribes in cash, gifts and stocks to buy government jobs; arranging jobs for people; and using intimidation or deception to hamper and impinge upon the democratic rights of delegates or committee members.

Table 8.1 **Corruption rankings in Asia**

| Rank | Country | 2007 | 2008 |
|---|---|---|---|
| 1 | Singapore | 1.13 | 1.07 |
| 2 | Hong Kong | 1.80 | 1.89 |
| 3 | Japan | 2.25 | 3.99 |
| 4 | South Korea | 5.65 | 4.64 |
| 5 | Macau | 3.30 | 5.84 |
| 6 | China | 7.98 | 6.16 |
| 7 | Taiwan | 6.55 | 6.47 |
| 8 | Malaysia | 6.37 | 6.70 |
| 9 | Philippines | 9.00 | 7.00 |
| 10 | Vietnam | 7.75 | 7.11 |
| 11 | India | 7.25 | 7.21 |
| 12 | Cambodia | – | 7.25 |
| 13 | Thailand | 8.00 | 7.63 |
| 14 | Indonesia | 7.98 | 8.32 |

Note: Figures are based on a survey of businessmen, focusing on corruption in 14 Asian countries, published by Political and Economic Risk Consultancy (PERC) in March 2009. On a scale of zero to ten, zero is the best possible score.
Source: Political and Economic Risk Consultancy

## Bribery and business

Bribery in China takes many forms, all of them illegal under local and international regulations. Legislation is now driving multinational enforcement. The Foreign Corrupt Practices Act (FCPA), which outlaws bribery of government officials worldwide and came into force in the United States back in 1977, is enjoying a new lease of life. The US Securities and Exchange Commission (SEC) is using it to fine companies that are registered, invested or listed in the United States for non-compliance in countries around the world. According to the China-based manager of one multinational company fined for FCPA violations, the SEC and the US Department of Justice closely scrutinise violators for signs of improvement and full compliance. Provisions within the Sarbanes-Oxley Act (2002) further strengthen accounting and financial reporting requirements for US firms. As a result, more than 90% of US businesses are worried about the potential for FCPA violations while doing business in China, according to a report published by accounting firm Deloitte in 2009.

US companies frequently point the finger at their European counterparts, complaining – as in the case of a US medical equipment manufacturer trying to sell its products in China – that European companies happily pay bribes to doctors or hospital managers in order to sell their products. (Since China's hospitals are state-run institutions, all hospital staff are "government officials" and therefore fall under FCPA obligations.) This may have been the case in some instances, but tighter enforcement of Europe's own anti-corruption legislation – notably the Convention on Combating Bribery of Foreign Public Officials in International Business Transactions created by the Paris-based Organisation for Economic Co-operation and Development (OECD) – has done much to eliminate this since its launch in 1999. Other legislation, such as the UK's Bribery Act (2010), sets even more stringent standards for companies registered, invested or listed in the UK in their dealings around the world.

Multinationals partnering with private Chinese companies should also be wary of potential skeletons in the closet. Between 2000 and 2004, the International Finance Corporation (IFC) invested $13m in Wumart Stores, a Beijing-based retail chain that was listed in Hong Kong in 2004. In 2006, Wumart's founder, Zhang Wenzhong, was arrested on suspicion of "improper" connections with disgraced former Beijing deputy mayor Liu Zhihua. In 2008, after two years in detention, Zhang was jailed for 18 years for misappropriation, bribery and fraud. Liu reportedly helped facilitate Wumart's early expansion in Beijing in the late 1990s.

149

## The ones that didn't get away

A number of multinationals have fallen foul of FCPA regulations in recent years. Actions have been brought against companies in the steel, software, telecoms, medical devices, trains and transmission lines and other sectors. Notable cases include the following:

- **UT Starcom.** In 2009 US telecoms company UT Starcom agreed to pay $3m in fines for bribes totalling $7m that were paid by its wholly owned China subsidiary to Chinese state officials between 2002 and 2007. These included 225 sightseeing trips to tourist destinations (described as "training programmes") such as New York, Hawaii and Las Vegas.
- **Control Components Inc.** In 2009, California-based CCI agreed to pay a $18.2m fine for systematic bribery committed in 30 countries (including China) between 2003 and 2007, including bribes paid to six Chinese companies.
- **Avery Dennison.** In 2009, Avery Dennison, a US maker of pressure-sensitive adhesive materials, was fined for paying bribes in China between 2004 and 2009. The SEC ordered the company to disgorge some $300,000, and the company agreed to a final judgment requiring it to pay a civil penalty of $200,000.
- **Lucent Technologies.** Between 2001 and 2004, US IT company Lucent Technologies expanded rapidly through various CDMA (code division multiple access) deals with China Unicom, a state telecoms company, raising total revenues of $90m (or 11% of the company's consolidated revenues). Then in 2004 allegations of bribery emerged, resulting in the dismissal of four executives in its China business, including the president and CEO, for FCPA violations. It emerged that between 2000 and 2003, Lucent paid for approximately 1,000 Chinese government officials to take trips to the United States, spending more than $10m on their travelling expenses. In 2007 Alcatel-Lucent, formed from a merger the previous year between Lucent and French technology company Alcatel, agreed to pay $2.5m in fines for the bribes paid by Lucent.
- **Siemens AG.** In 2006, German telecoms company Siemens came under investigation at home for global bribery of up to $42m, including bribery in the bidding process for a public hospital in north-eastern Jilin province. Siemens had already been in China for ten years. Siemens was eventually fined $800m by the SEC, though total fines by US and Germany regulatory authorities reached $1.65 billion.
- **DPC.** In 2005, DPC, the world's largest manufacturer of medical diagnostic equipment, was accused by the US Judicial Department of paying $1.6m in bribes to Chinese state-owned hospitals between 1991 and 2002 in an attempt to convince the hospitals to switch to DPC products. The company was fined $4.9m.

### Financial crime: fraud and embezzlement

Multinationals setting up operations in China often discover that internal controls are weak, company records incomplete (particularly given high employee turnover rates) and the compliance environment not particularly robust. In many cases concepts such as corporate governance, fiduciary duty and business ethics have yet to evolve. One multinational manager in Shanghai says:

> The Chinese have being doing business with family and friends for hundreds of years ... so they have further to go in complying with the FCPA.

It should come as no surprise, then, that related-party transactions are commonplace and bribery in commercial dealings routine. Making things worse are the actions of multinational companies' senior managers who, having a limited understanding of local conditions and the language, opt to leave operational decisions to their local Chinese managers. The head of a Japanese manufacturing operation in China who received allegations of fraud within its organisation in southern China discovered that its most senior local manager – a long-serving Japanese-speaking employee who had previously lived in Japan – was defrauding the company on a massive scale by selling surplus, reject and returned products in the market. The Japanese senior managers' ignorance of Chinese and English had forced them to rely too heavily on one individual within the company.

Multinational companies that have been in China for decades are also targets. The manager of a US retailer received poison-pen letters alleging fraud by senior sales managers within the company. It subsequently emerged that a network of local managers who had known each other since childhood were defrauding the company by setting up shell distribution companies through which they channelled products en route to the retailer. The manager's company was just one in a succession of multinational companies that had been defrauded using exactly the same method. Afraid to disrupt its business even more than it already had and risk anti-foreign feeling in the office, the manager was obliged to let the culprits resign without attempting to press charges.

Unfortunately, if fraud is uncovered, the local legal system is not always of great assistance. China's written laws are generally good, and the police are typically dedicated and "clean", especially in big urban areas. However, interpretation of laws can vary dramatically from one jurisdiction to another and white-collar crime is not a high priority. Further reducing the chance of success is the fact that the judiciary is underdeveloped and not beyond political influence – judges are CPC appointees, and are usually not trained lawyers. Even enforcement is problematic: on average only half of all court rulings in China are successfully enforced.

The government has sought to make examples of officials accused of fraud and corruption. In 2006 the head of the SFDA was executed for approving untested medicine, including an antibiotic that killed at least ten people, in exchange for cash payments. Businessmen have been targeted too. The former chairman of Guangdong Kelon Electrical Holdings, once China's biggest refrigerator-maker, was sentenced to 12 years in prison for falsifying and withholding information and for embezzlement of up to $49m. On a smaller scale, a man was sentenced to death in north-eastern China in 2007 for defrauding investors in a would-be ant-breeding scheme. The man had promised returns of up to 60% for investors who purchased ant-breeding kits from two companies he ran. The insects were to be used in traditional medicinal wines, herbal remedies and aphrodisiacs. The business attracted more than 10,000 investors between 2002 and 2005, when investigators finally shut it down. The closure set off a panic among small-time investors, who saw their life savings disappear overnight.

The authorities, concerned about social unrest, have come down hard on fake investments and pyramid schemes.

## Achieving compliance in China

From an operational perspective, many executives see corruption as a cost of doing business in China. Yet it is possible to do business without resorting to bribes – which is just as well, given the increasingly bright spotlight being directed at multinationals and their affiliates in China.

The key to effective compliance is prevention. To comply with the FCPA companies should consider establishing corporate compliance programmes in a bid to raise awareness within their organisations and so minimise the risk of improper payments being made. According to the local head of an international risk consultancy in Shanghai, most compliance programmes comprise two parts: a clear, concise corporate compliance document made available to all local staff (who should be tested for their knowledge of the guidelines); and training of all staff (particularly those in sales, marketing, distribution and accounts) to raise awareness of the principal compliance issues.

Many multinational companies operate global compliance lines as part of their FCPA or OECD obligations. Yet many such lines are ineffective. One western company found that it had received no calls whatsoever via its China line for over a year. Closer inspection revealed that workers were unwilling to call an overseas number and in any case did not believe that the line was operated by entirely independent parties, and some callers had been confronted with an English-speaking operator. The solution was to set up a separate local line with Chinese-speaking staff that operated as a link to the global compliance line. The company launched the new local number with an awareness campaign for "speaking up", advertising the compliance line number on posters around the factory and offices, on credit-card size cards distributed to individual workers and on official receipts sent to the company's partners and suppliers. The result was a huge increase in the line's use and the exposure of several fraudulent operations with the help of anonymous whistle-blowers.

Establishing effective compliance programmes for multinational operations has become a priority for multinational companies wishing to avoid these problems – with more than a nudge from the increasingly stringent regulations created in the wake of numerous well-publicised corporate frauds. In mid-2004, the US Sentencing Commission revised its sentencing guidelines, which require US companies' domestic and global operations to enhance internal compliance to help prevent and detect corporate malfeasance. The Sentencing Commission's original guidelines included seven minimum criteria to be used as a benchmark for an effective compliance programme. The 2004 revisions flesh out these criteria significantly, and link them with a series of similar Sarbanes-Oxley Act requirements. The revised elements are as follows:

- **Management responsibility and corporate culture.** Corporate executives – including the board of directors – are required to take an active role in promoting a culture of compliance and exercise oversight of the company's compliance programme. The tone from the top is crucial to the success of anti-corruption initiatives.
- **Due diligence to prevent malfeasance.** This common-sense requirement requires organisations to exercise due diligence to detect and avoid engagements or relationships that could prove problematic, whether they are prospective·business partners, acquisition targets, suppliers, distributors or management hires.
- **Effective communication and training.** Employees need to be regularly trained (at least annually) regarding compliance issues and surveyed to ensure appropriate lessons have been learnt.
- **Monitoring, auditing, evaluation.** Regular monitoring is another area that is often overlooked or deliberately avoided. Yet the

### Chasing naked officials

The term "naked officials" was coined in 2009 to describe party officials whose families have moved overseas (generally with the help of embezzled funds) while the officials continue to work in China – though with a visa for the country in question close to hand.

In 2010 the National Bureau of Corruption Prevention and Ministry of Supervision announced plans to set up a system to monitor naked officials and stricter requirements for CPC cadres to provide detailed personal and family information. In the same year, the CPC Central Committee issued a new 52-point ethics code for party cadres, outlawing activities such as accepting cash or financial instruments as gifts, and using influence to benefit the business operations of family members, friends or associates.

Enforcement is also a priority. In early 2010 the Supreme People's Court issued new regulations aimed at preventing the abuse of judicial powers and installed nearly 25,000 anti-corruption supervisors in 2,400 courts across the country. The regulations provide for tougher penalties for crimes committed by judges, from run-of-the-mill bribe taking to the less common adultery with litigants or their relatives. The new rules follow the jailing for life of Huang Songyou, former vice-president of the Supreme People's Court, who embezzled funds and accepted bribes totalling more than Rmb3.9m ($574,000) between 2005 and 2008.

Lastly, the government is seeking to audit the use of public funds more rigorously, particularly those used in construction and infrastructure. The revised Audit Law (effective May 1st 2010) allows auditors to monitor fiscal funds used by public bodies and by other companies and projects.

### The UK Bribery Act: not just for the British

The UK's dogged reliance on fragmented and complex laws (one of which dates back to the 1880s) finally came to an end in 2010 with the passage of the long-delayed Bribery Act. A quantum leap in regulatory terms, the act is the most stringent to date of any country's laws on foreign bribery, according to John Bray, an anti-corruption specialist at Control Risks, a specialist risk consultancy. Unlike the Foreign Corrupt Practices Act, the Bribery Act covers bribes paid to private companies as well as foreign officials, and includes facilitation payments to speed up routine government procedures such as customs clearances. It also underlines the need for an effective compliance programme by introducing a new offence of "corporate failure to prevent bribery". The act applies not only to UK companies and individuals, but also to foreign companies incorporated in the UK, as well as foreign citizens who are ordinarily resident there.

majority of the problems that employers encounter could have been dramatically minimised if they had discovered malfeasance earlier.

- **Reporting systems.** This revision requires implementation and promotion of anonymous reporting systems so that malfeasance or compliance violations can be brought to the attention of management. By encouraging a culture of "speaking up" through anonymous hotlines, senior management can learn about and respond swiftly to such issues.
- **Accountability and corrective actions.** Corporations must take disciplinary or legal action when suspected malfeasance is detected, and make improvements to internal controls to prevent recurrences. Most importantly, policies must be in place outlining what constitutes a violation, levels of offence and measures the company may take in response.
- **Regular assessment of compliance performance and risk.** Lastly, the guidelines require a continuous assessment of the compliance risks faced by corporations.

According to a report published by the Association of Certified Fraud Examiners (ACFE), unofficial tip-offs (from either inside or outside the organisation) provide the most important source of information about non-compliance. Yet although internal audit departments are often tasked with investigating suspected frauds, internal audits uncover fewer than 20% of instances of non-compliance, according to the ACFE.

## Summary

- **Write it down.** Create, maintain and update codes of conduct.
- **Live and breathe it.** Make all employees sign codes of conduct and provide relevant training to make sure that they fully understand the principal regulations.
- **Zero tolerance.** Multinationals need to demonstrate zero-tolerance policies towards fraud and corruption by acting swiftly and decisively to remove fraudsters from their organisations.

# 9 Corporate governance and social responsibility

Reputation arrives on foot and leaves on a horse.

Anonymous

**M**ultinational investment and heightened demands from companies' headquarters for transparency in global operations have come as a shock to many local managers and state-owned enterprises with foreign partners. Traditional business practices are being scrutinised through an international microscope, with far-reaching consequences for the way business is conducted in many sectors. This chapter examines the regulatory changes that are reducing manipulation in the financial markets and raising overall levels of compliance and transparency.

## Principles of corporate governance

What is corporate governance? Simply defined, it is the set of processes, policies and regulations affecting the way a company is run. It includes the relationship between a company and its shareholders, from directors, managers and employees to suppliers, customers and the wider community. Corporate governance focuses on ensuring the accountability of senior management in achieving the goals of a company in economically efficient and ethically sound ways.

The principles of corporate governance include the following:

- **Shareholder rights and treatment.** Companies should respect the rights of all shareholders and help them to exercise those rights through effective communication of information.
- **Board roles and responsibilities.** The board of a company should contain independent non-executive directors capable of understanding the business and where necessary challenging management decisions and performance.
- **Integrity and ethical behaviour.** Companies operating to high ethical standards benefit in terms of risk management and public relations. A company code of conduct that is regularly updated and effectively communicated to all stakeholders helps to promote

ethical and responsible decision-making and so minimise the risk of non-compliance with international anti-corruption legislation.

◼ **Disclosure and transparency.** Companies should communicate to all shareholders the roles and responsibilities of board members and senior management to ensure a level of accountability.

◼ **Independent financial reporting.** Companies should put in place procedures to ensure independent and accurate reporting of their financial accounts by respected external auditors.

Growing public demand and regulatory pressure for greater accountability among listed companies means that senior management must pay closer attention to these principles. The good news is that in doing so companies also make themselves more attractive and trustworthy partners to foreign investors. By contrast, companies with poor governance can suffer from any or all of the following problems: lack of confidentiality; poor protection of company assets, including intellectual property; conflicts of interest; non-compliance with regulations; and a lack of trust in relationships with employees and external partners.

Companies that demonstrate high levels of transparency, disclosure and mutual respect within their China operations can benefit practically from minimising or even eliminating corruption, bribery and fraud in their operations – ensuring that they are in compliance with the Foreign Corrupt Practices Act (FCPA), OECD regulations, the UK Bribery Act and a host of other rigorously enforced international regulations.

In China good governance programmes now usually form part of a multinational company's core business strategy. Many of the due diligence precautions that foreign investors are advised to take when assessing acquisition targets should be applied within the company itself. Pre-employment background checks, for example, help reduce problems of fraud and bribery, as do effectively communicated codes of conduct. Organisation charts add to transparency and highlight reporting lines.

## Legal framework for corporate governance structures

As in other areas of China's legislative landscape, the legal framework covering corporate governance for foreign-invested enterprises (FIEs) in China is in a state of evolution as the government seeks to strengthen relevant structures and fiduciary duties, particularly for listed companies. FIEs historically operated a simple governance structure, usually comprising a board of directors (typically chaired by the legal representative) and a management structure led by a general manager, who ran the business on a day-to-day basis. However, the Opinions on Several Issues Concerning the Application of the Laws on Examination, Approval and Registration of Companies with Foreign Investment (2006) now require wholly owned foreign enterprises (WOFEs) to operate the governance structures set out for domestic companies in the Company Law (2006). Directors and senior officers in foreign-invested enterprises (FIEs) must act honestly and diligently on behalf of their company in exercising their fiduciary duties, and can face personal liability for failing to do so. Under anti-money-laundering laws, directors and officers can also be held liable for taking bribes, unauthorised lending, fund misappropriation and illegally disclosing company secrets.

Foreign investors partnered with Chinese-listed firms face a number of other regulations issued by the China Securities Regulatory Commission (CSRC), one of the main bodies responsible for regulating the country's stockmarkets. These rules, which are intended to help listed companies create independent director mechanisms, are:

- the Guideline Regarding Independent Directors in Listing Companies (2002);
- the Guideline Regarding the Restructuring of Companies Before their Initial Public Offerings (2003);
- Guidelines for Corporate Governance of Listing Companies (2003).

Foreign investors partnered with domestic companies (including state entities) should also note the Temporary Regulations on the Implementation of an Accountability System for Senior Cadres of the Party and Government (2009), which makes CPC or government officials responsible for mishandling social protests, and the Regulations on the Integrity of Leaders of State-owned Enterprises (2004, updated 2009), which toughens up penalties for officials engaged in misconduct. This includes doing business with immediate family members and (for the first time) with persons of "special relationships" – a term not used in the previous document. These special relationships are intended primarily to cover mistresses of the principal operators who have often been the recipients of the fruits in frauds and other malfeasance.

## Corporate social responsibility programmes

Corporate social responsibility (CSR) in China takes many forms but is generally defined as duty of care to employees and the community, namely: health, safety and the environment (HSE); and community relations. HSE forms part of a company's responsibilities to provide a safe and carefully regulated working environment for its staff. This should extend far beyond the often skeletal labour laws and regulations in place in countries such as China, and foreign investors can benefit from applying international-standard HSE measures to incorporate their suppliers, distributors and other affiliates.

Companies increasingly seek to strengthen their position in their operating community by improving the overall standards of living for all residents in the communities in which they do business. This can be building local schools or subsidising specific educational programmes, from primary through to college level, building essential infrastructure, such as roads to link communities to the outside world or clinics providing basic health care, and providing technical assistance to local farmers seeking to maximise their crop yield.

Multinational companies have often established CSR programmes for emerging markets that they also deploy in China. Some are highly effective examples of best practice; others sink without trace. Those that do not succeed – such as a village school funded by a US manufacturer that was set up in an area already well served by local schools simply because it was run by a local government official known to the company's local joint-venture partner – fail to define the programme's goals and its viability. Initiatives should also be broadly aligned with the sectors or direction of the company concerned. For example, health-care companies might consider setting up community health-care programmes in remote rural areas. This would provide a rationale for the programmes and develop a relevant profile for the company in the local community.

Foreign investors considering CSR initiatives in China should consider the following:

- **Tailor programmes for China.** Multinational companies should be prepared, if necessary, to tailor global CSR programmes to local realities and needs in China. A series of smaller local initiatives may be more suitable than an ambitious programme run through central government with the accompanying red tape that might involve.
- **Involve senior management.** Senior management should be deeply involved in CSR programmes and in promoting CSR messages. A company's corporate communications division might be responsible for running the CSR programme, but senior management should be seen to be working closely with the team to set the tone from the top.

- **Choose the right project.** Multinational companies should identify a community's needs; it is best not to build a school in a community that has schools but lacks a hospital. Develop projects for migrant workers if most of the workforce come from this labour pool.
- **Involve company staff.** If most employees come from the local neighbourhood, participation by local staff can drive a project forward. Similarly, employees with a personal interest in the projects in question can be recruited.
- **Recognise contributions from staff and company CSR achievements.** Annual events such as banquets featuring award ceremonies encourage further participation, build company spirit and act as a corporate networking opportunity for staff from different offices.
- **Align CSR programmes with government plans and goals.** By addressing tasks outlined in the central government's Eleventh Five-Year Plan (a regularly updated blueprint for economic development) and provincial government objectives, companies can demonstrate their long-term commitment to China and the reciprocal nature of their relationship.
- **Maintain contact with company's head office.** CSR managers in China should have regular and direct contact with the company's head office CSR function to make sure their programmes fit central values and strategies.

Foreign investors can also choose to execute their CSR initiatives in partnership with international or domestic non-government organisations (NGOs). By working with NGOs, companies can align themselves with worthwhile programmes, thus cutting out much of the red tape and avoiding beginners' mistakes that starting from scratch may involve. This approach requires a carefully articulated message from multinational companies to NGOs, some of which appreciate financial and logistical support but may be wary of partnering with such companies. (For a list of international NGOs operating in China, see the China Development Brief at www.chinadevelopmentbrief.com.) Domestic NGOs may be more difficult partners because they are often government-backed, which can slow down programme progress. The China Association for NGO Co-operation (CANGO, www.cango.org) can help companies find the right CSR partners. Both international and domestic NGOs can provide organised access to charitable programmes. These can be continuous or event-driven, such as the Sichuan earthquake or the HIV outbreak in Henan.

Other local partners are also worth considering. In a country where education is highly prized and well-educated staff are sought after, companies should consider developing education-related CSR initiatives. Many companies sponsor local students through college, or provide funding for new classrooms, furniture, personal computers or textbooks.

## Summary

- **Lower the risk of corruption.** Effective corporate governance mitigates the risk of corruption, deflects the attention of the anti-corruption bodies and ultimately improves business efficiency.
- **A cleaner company is worth more.** Local companies will buy into corporate governance, even if it is only a way to raise pre-IPO or pre-transaction valuations.

# 10 Future China

The only constant is change.

Heraclitus of Ephesus (circa 535–475BC)

Over the next 5–10 years China faces enormous challenges. Three are especially daunting:

- **Achieving balanced and sustained economic development in order to strengthen social stability and thus ensure the regime's political survival.** This requires initiatives on numerous fronts, including incentives for greater innovation to move the economy up the value chain and thus reduce its dependence on the export model, and strengthening the central government's relationship with provincial administrations, thereby reducing the corrosive effects of official corruption at the local level.
- **Securing the resources and assets the country needs to fuel and grow its economy.** This will require unprecedented direct investment in all parts of the world as well as an increasingly nuanced and sophisticated foreign policy befitting an emerging global superpower.
- **Addressing the issue of environmental degradation, notably climate change, as the country becomes not only the world's largest manufacturer but also its largest consumer market.** Failure to do so will undermine economic growth efforts and increase social instability, which could damage foreign investor confidence and complicate the operating environment for multinational business.

## Balancing and sustaining economic growth

In 2006 the CPC Central Committee formally adopted Secretary-General Hu Jintao's proposal to "build a harmonious socialist society" (see Chapter 2), specifying that social concerns such as the yawning income gap between urban rich and rural poor, access to decent education and effective health care, endemic official corruption and environmental pollution should all be placed on a par with economic growth.

Jane Duckett, professor of Chinese and comparative politics at Glasgow

University, has doubts about the ability of the Chinese central leadership, no matter how well intentioned, to overcome the country's systemic problems:[1]

> The commitment of top leaders makes an enormous difference in terms of putting social policies on the agenda and securing central government investment, and so it is to be hoped that the next generation leadership will retain a clearly stated pro-poor, pro-rural focus. But even China's powerful top leaders will find it difficult to overcome the problems created by a fiscally decentralised governance system and urban-biased, pro-coastal policies initiated in the 1990s: policies tend to be path dependent particularly if their beneficiaries are powerful. Efforts to change the economic growth priorities of local governments – such as including social development in performance indicators – have so far had limited impact. This may be in part because it is at present unclear how deep the top leadership's commitment is to fundamentally tackling the rural-urban divide.
>
> Many of the endemic problems in the Chinese economy today – massive pollution, corruption, inefficient capital deployment, land grabs – cannot be tackled without meaningful institutional reforms, particularly reforms of Chinese political governance. So far, the policy rhetoric is encouraging. The issue is whether the current leaders will truly follow their policy rhetoric to its logical conclusion – empowering people through political reforms.

### Innovation for the nation

Foreign-invested innovation will play a part in China's efforts to move up the value chain. China overtook the United States and India in 2007 to become the top global destination for research and development, according to a UN report published the following year. The report claimed that China had roughly 1,000 R&D centres, most of them in the technology sector.[2] Zinnov Management Consultants, a research firm, puts the figure slightly lower at 920 multinational-invested R&D centres in China, compared with 671 in India. Motorola alone had invested $300m in 19 facilities by 2008. Some 88% of China's high-tech exports are manufactured by foreign-invested enterprises, and the proportion is increasing.

Yet while innovation will help China's economy grow and mature in the long term, the main drivers for the next 5–10 years will remain low manufacturing costs and a growing consumer market. Although the country's competitiveness has been eroded by rising land and labour costs in traditional manufacturing regions (notably southern China) and the emergence of alternative production sites in neighbouring countries such as Vietnam and Indonesia, China continues to offer low-cost manufacturing in inland regions that are increasingly supported by massive investment in infrastructure. This continuing attractiveness, combined with an emerging consumer market of unprecedented proportions, makes a compelling case for China.

However, low-cost manufacturing in inland areas brings the same problems that used to exist elsewhere for foreign companies sourcing goods from Chinese manufacturers: poor communications, variable product quality and the general hassles of dealing with a partner inexperienced in sourcing and global trade. Consequently, growing numbers of foreign companies are choosing to source from comparatively well-established Chinese manufacturers that represent better value for money in the long run.

### Centre versus local

Since 1949 China's central government has rigorously exercised its authority over the provincial administrations, ensuring adherence to central policies and preventing the emergence of regional fiefdoms by rotating local party and military heads on a regular basis. Yet China's vast size and cultural diversity complicate this task, giving some of the more distant provinces a surprising degree of economic autonomy – particularly when they are by nature more freewheeling, entrepreneurial and strategically located, such as the southern provinces of Guangdong, Fujian and Hainan.

The government recognises that it must allow its diverse regions to play to their economic strengths while keeping a lid on the sources of potential instability that could weaken its control. Although political leaders in Beijing have occasionally used the south's commercial flair to further their own campaigns – Deng's "Southern Tour" of Shenzhen and other cities in 1992 was responsible for rekindling the market reform process in the face of conservative opposition in the Politburo – the central government has tended to keep the southern provinces on a tight leash in the knowledge that economic freedom brings with it official corruption and an often "creative" enforcement of business laws and regulations. A Chinese proverb, "the mountains are high and the emperor is far away", dating back to the Qing dynasty (1644–1911), is often used with reference to southern China. The region has certainly had its fair share of big corruption scandals, involving both government and party leaders, from huge smuggling operations in the mid-1990s to bribery scandals involving senior officials in Fujian in 2009 and Chongqing in 2010. Yet corruption is not restricted to more remote regions. As well as the Chen Liangyu case in Shanghai, the CPC boss in Beijing, Chen Xitong, was jailed in 1995 on charges of corruption and bribery.

The central government will continue to take the good with the bad: granting the autonomy that allows China's economic engine to keep firing on all cylinders, while continuing to crack down on the accompanying problems of corruption, bribery and poor legal and regulatory enforcement. The risk it runs is the corrosive effect that corruption and the abuse of power have on the image of the government and the CPC, which needs to justify its legitimacy as the ruling party. The central leadership will continue to tread this fine line between autonomy and control.

When it comes to political and social freedoms, no such autonomy is in evidence. The government believes that only strong central government can maintain national cohesion. Certainly, the country's vast size and often harsh terrain complicate the task, particularly given that many of the country's most politically sensitive regions lie in border areas and that it is not on especially good terms with some of its neighbours. The regions of Xinjiang, Tibet, Inner Mongolia and Yunnan, Guizhou and Guangxi in the south-west contain many of China's non-Han ethnic minority communities, a number of which resent what they see as Han suppression of their ethnic, religious and cultural identities. Poor government or the abuse of power at the local level exacerbates these tensions, leading to violent protests such as those that have occurred in Xinjiang (particularly in 2009) and Tibet. The central government is hoping that improvements in living conditions for these minority populations will offset restrictions in political, cultural and religious activities.

## Going out: China as a global superpower

China's emergence as a global superpower has been swift, and was given an extra push by the global financial crisis, which resulted in US and European manufacturers expanding further in China in an effort to cut operating costs. China's economy cannot keep up its growth without more input from the outside world.

Since 2005 the open door, which since 1979 had swung inwards to allow foreign investors into the country, has started to swing both ways as Chinese investors look overseas for the assets and markets they need to sustain economic development at home. China has three principal requirements:

◪ Natural resources, predominantly oil, to fuel economic growth. It started acquiring natural resources in Asia before moving to Africa, the Middle East, Latin America and elsewhere. Its attempted acquisition of Unocal, a US oil company, in 2005 scared the US government and led to a bid rejection on "strategic grounds".

◪ Strategic assets to help make the Chinese economy more innovative and so move it up the value chain. Hence Lenovo's acquisition of IBM's personal computer division in 2004, Nanjing Automotive's acquisition of ailing UK carmaker MG Rover in 2006 and Geely's acquisition of Swedish car brand Volvo from Ford in 2010.

◪ New markets for exports as the market pressure on major domestic manufacturers operating on razor-thin margins intensifies.

China is performing surprisingly well considering its lack of experience in mergers and acquisitions. It has of course made mistakes: following its failed bid for Unocal in 2005, it lost heavily in an unfortunately timed investment in financial services company Blackstone in 2007 at the end of the buy-out boom. Its lack of international experience and its diplomatic insensitivity are evident in some African states where it has invested, for example importing Chinese labour rather than using local workers, thereby alienating local communities.

Yet China is learning from these mistakes, rapidly becoming a more savvy negotiator in M&A and appreciating the importance of a positive international image. As part of this public-relations campaign, the government is taking on more international responsibilities as befits a major global player. For example, in 2009 it sent naval vessels to the Gulf of Aden to help international forces in the fight against maritime piracy off the coast of Somalia. This was the first time Chinese ships had travelled through these waters since the 13th century.

Through these experiences China is gaining the confidence to become a global superpower. It is selectively asserting its authority more strongly and frequently, both in its own region (such as in its relations with old enemies India and Vietnam) and on the global stage (such as in its demands to be treated as an equal partner by the United States and in pushing for greater voting rights at the IMF to match its increasing contributions). The country's growing confidence is evident in its increasingly robust protection of its national interests, especially strategically important industries, sometimes to the cost of multinational companies. In early 2010 US internet giant Google found itself increasingly edged out of the mainland search-engine market after relocating its Chinese web-search site to Hong Kong in a bid to retain uncensored search capabilities.

However, such incidents are rare. China's agenda is primarily commercial, driven by the need to keep fuelling and developing its economy. The government is keen to make the most of its investments and understands that the country's emerging role as a global superpower requires a more nuanced and sophisticated foreign policy. Its integration with the world economy will continue to accelerate, raising its international profile and thereby increasing its responsibility as a global player. China's flexibility and pragmatism, visible in the country's continual transformations, form a convincing argument against future scenarios of doom and gloom. China is too dependent on the world to bite the hand that feeds it, according to James Kynge.[3]

## Healing the environment

The Chinese government names economic growth as its top priority, with environmental protection following close behind. Yet one is being achieved at the cost of the other, as no-holds-barred economic growth continues to wreak havoc on the natural environment. China's major cities are among the most polluted in the world. A World Bank report puts the economic cost of China's air and water pollution at 3–8% of GDP. If current trends continue, its environmental future will be bleak, with worrying consequences for the living standards of its people and operating conditions for foreign investors.

China is already the world's largest emitter of greenhouse gases measured on an annual basis, even though its per-head emissions remain modest. Significantly, it contributes around two-thirds of the global annual increase in carbon-dioxide emissions. The realisation that climate change could have worrying social and economic consequences at home is prompting the government to adopt a more thoughtful and long-term approach to the environment than in the past. The effects of climate change within the country are evident: flooding in the south, extended droughts in the north and extreme weather conditions generally. The scarcity of water in northern rivers and the flooding of southern rivers are expected to increase in the first half of this century, raising the possibility of environmental protests and potential conflict arising from a scarcity of water and other natural resources.

Research published by the Chinese Academy of Sciences (CAS) in the *Chinese Science Bulletin* suggests a link between climate change and periods of social unrest and conflict in Chinese history.[4] Some 70–80% of conflicts, and most changes of dynasty, were found to occur during "cold phases", leading the researchers to the conclusion that cold weather reduced land productivity and resources, thereby creating and fuelling conflict. Although the correlation may not be strong, few would argue that climate change and the subsequent depletion of resources add another variable to global stability.

One of China's immediate concerns is the stability of its agricultural sector, which employs more than half the population. A predicted 5–10% reduction in overall crop productivity by 2030, largely because of a declining water supply and increasing desertification in the north, would seriously affect the country's long-term food security. Another concern is the increasing frequency of tropical storms, which have increased flooding in low-lying areas, typically the highly populated, economically developed deltas of the Pearl, Yangtze and Yellow rivers in the south, east and north respectively. The vulnerability of these crucial regions to storm-induced flooding and from a longer-term rise in sea level is worrying.

Aware of its role in global warming, China has set ambitious targets to reduce energy intensity and carbon emissions. (Energy intensity is a measure of the energy efficiency of a country's economy. It is calculated as units of energy per unit of GDP. High energy intensity therefore indicates a high price or cost of converting energy into GDP, whereas low energy intensity indicates a lower price or cost of converting energy into GDP.)

It aimed for a 20% reduction in energy use per unit of GDP between 2005 and 2010, and a 40–45% reduction in carbon emissions per unit of GDP between 2005 and 2020. Official data suggest that it is on track to reach its energy-intensity target, though questions have been raised about the reliability of the data.

China's continuing reliance on fossil fuels at least until 2030 as a means to power its economy will keep its carbon dioxide emissions high, even taking into account the development of low- or zero-emission coal technologies. Yet it has also embraced renewable energy and demonstrated real progress in the wind and solar power sectors, accounting for 35% of the global market for photovoltaic cells by 2007. While economic growth will remain China's top priority, the adoption of low-carbon technologies suggests that it may eventually become an ally rather than an adversary in the fight against climate change. China's willingness to take tough environmental measures at home and its increased participation in global environmental issues will not only strengthen its international image among countries still apprehensive about its intentions, but also will demonstrate its growing maturity and commitment to responsibility as the next global superpower.

## Some scenarios

There are three broad scenarios facing China over the next few years:

- continuing political and economic stability (70% probability);
- gradual erosion of economic stability and political legitimacy, fuelling social unrest and damaging the business climate, but with no regime change (25%);
- economic crisis and/or social upheaval causing political conflict and ultimately regime change, derailing economic growth (5%).

### Scenario 1: continuing political and economic stability.

Despite initial concerns that its economic stability would be undermined by its reliance on exports, China has emerged largely intact from the global economic crisis. Crucial to this has been a massive state stimulus plan and pre-crisis economic strategy to climb up the value chain and consolidate fragmented industries while investing in cheaper inland provinces. Inflation remains a concern, but the country's good fiscal health gives policymakers a range of levers to tweak.

Potential problems include the income gap, unemployment and official corruption, any of which could cause widespread social unrest but would not be sufficient to bring down the government. China's one-party system can survive alongside economic growth, though that growth will need to be close to the forecast GDP growth rates of 7–9% for the next few years. The government remains committed to a market economy but fears of foreign competition persist and, as Andrew Gilholm of Control Risks says, the country "continues to view free-market economics as a means and not an end". Yet while growing pressure on China's political and economic system will ultimately force change in the long term, continuing stability and a positive business climate remain the most likely scenario for the next five years at least.

### Scenario 2: gradual erosion of political and economic stability

This less likely scenario could be triggered by a prolonged economic slump with low levels of GDP, falling foreign investment and a widespread loss of confidence sparking significant social unrest and political instability. In this scenario, a succession of policy errors combined with external shocks leads to a serious economic slowdown that cripples major banks, destroys business confidence and affects the livelihoods of large sections of the population. As growth slows and joblessness rises, the welfare state comes under pressure and social tensions across the country lead to protests and disturbances, which the security forces vigorously quash. Foreign investment falls away and international criticism focuses on those companies that keep doing business in or with China. The regime holds on to power by appealing to popular nationalism, further damaging foreign investor confidence, but continues to push economic development. As a result, China is unlikely to return to scenario 1 and will probably decline further as described in scenario 3.

## Scenario 3: economic crisis, social upheaval and political collapse
The least likely scenario, while hardly conceivable within the next few years, will merit greater consideration in the long term if the central government fails to maintain its fine balance between authoritarian control and economic development. Even so, a collapse of government authority and subsequent regime change will be only a remote possibility caused by far-reaching external and internal shocks such as a global oil crisis, a pandemic or an international incident arising from a military confrontation. In this scenario, economic collapse ensues, sparking nationwide unrest and a loss of control by the security forces. A political split in the leadership prompts hardliners to attempt unsuccessfully to restore control through the use of military and paramilitary force. Foreign business confidence is shattered as the country descends into political chaos for a period.

# Notes and references

## City classification

1 *Far Eastern Economic Review*, "Hunting for Fortune In Postcrisis China", January 9th 2009.

## 1 Making it work in China

1 The term BRIC was coined in 2001 by Jim O'Neill, chief economist at Goldman Sachs, to describe the emerging markets of Brazil, Russia, India and China.

2 The US-China Business Council (USBC) is a private, not-for-profit organisation with more than 200 US corporate members that do business with China. Founded in 1973, it aims to expand the US-China commercial relationship to the benefit of its membership and the US economy in general.

3 Economist Intelligence Unit, *Business China: Is China less risky than the US?*, April 13th 2009. According to the Economist Intelligence Unit, indicators of underlying vulnerability include: instability; state history; corruption; ethnic fragmentation; trust in institutions; status of minorities; history of political instability; proclivity to labour unrest; level of social provision; a country's neighbourhood; regime type (full democracy, "flawed" democracy, hybrid or authoritarian); and the interaction of regime type with political factionalism. Indicators of economic distress are growth in incomes, unemployment and level of income per head.

4 Grigg, W.N., *New American*, May 16th 2005. "Global Motors: decades of corrupt collusion with the foreign-aid industry have left General Motors, once the colossus of the auto industry, facing extinction."

5 In *Mr China: A Memoir* (Constable & Robinson, 2004), Tim Clissold summarises Asimco's experience in China. Asimco invested in beer plants and car manufacturing in the 1990s, hoping to rationalise and consolidate Chinese companies operating in the same sectors in China. It did not achieve this and local companies absorbed Asimco's capital, leaving it with zero return. According to John Williams, who has lived and worked in Beijing for the past 20 years, this was the result of poor understanding of the market and of the management structures of

Chinese companies, and failure to identify the right partners.

6 Quoted in Clifton, R., *Brands and Branding*, Profile Books, 2009.

7 Issued to all foreign residents and visitors, foreign exchange certificates (FECs or *waihuiquan*) were a means of collecting hard currency for the Chinese government when its own currency, the renminbi, was not convertible. FECs had previously been used in the Soviet Union.

8 *Xiaomaibu* contain a select group of global brands with the logistical clout to grow and maintain enormous, sophisticated distribution networks: Wrigley's chewing gum, Procter & Gamble's Pantene shampoo, Coca-Cola.

9 Taiwanese companies have invested an estimated $150 billion in China over the past 30 years, despite sporadic political tensions between the two countries. Today more than 1m Taiwanese nationals (some 5% of Taiwan's population) live in China, concentrated in areas such as Kunshan, a centre for electronics manufacturing just west of Shanghai.

10 Euromonitor International puts Pepsi at 44.5% and Coca-Cola 47.3%, though Pepsi disputes these figures.

11 The *Book of Songs*, containing 305 poems, is part of the Five Classics (*Wu Jing*) used by Confucianism as a basis for study: *Book of Changes*; *Book of Songs*; *Book of Rites*; *Book of History*; *Spring and Autumn Annals*.

12 *Blat* first appeared in the Soviet Union in connection with using official connections to make black-market deals. The word may have originated from the Yiddish *blatt*, meaning a piece of paper.

13 Loosely related to *guanxi*, *wasta* is an Arabic expression referring to the traditional use of personal connections or influence to cut through red tape in order to get things done. It is believed to stem from *wasit*, meaning medium, intermediary or middleman.

14 Pye, L., *Asian Power and Politics*, Belknap Press of Harvard University Press, 1985, p. 292.

15 Pye, L., *Chinese Commercial Negotiating Style*, Oelgeschlager, Gunn & Hain, 1982.

16 The political and corporate networks underpinning much of business in China stem back to Beijing's Qinghua University (China's equivalent of the Massachusetts Institute of Technology), a centre for academic excellence with a history of radicalism. Qinghua (also known by its old romanised name Tsinghua) was a breeding ground for the Cultural Revolution where the Red Guards were first formed at a secondary school attached to the university. Qinghua became a source of "red engineers" (a term originally taken from the Soviet Union): a source of both political and technical power for China. Many of the

red engineers who went on to become technocrats in the leadership of the Chinese Communist Party (CCP) studied there. Their children are known as *taizi* or princelings (the children of high-ranking technocrats or revolutionary heroes). There are seven major *taizidang* (princeling groups) based largely on the families of individual senior leaders: Ye Jianying family, Hu Yaobang family, Deng Xiaoping family, Wang Zhen family, Chen Yun family, Tao Zhu family, Yang Shangkun family. The CCP's organisation department limited the number of *taizi* from each family occupying high-ranking government positions, though there are no such limits within the corporate world. The fourth-generation *taizi* cannot depend on their own political credentials and are generally less secure than the *taizi* of the previous generation. (Cheng Li, *China's Leaders: The New Generation*, Rowman & Littlefield Publishers, 2001, p. 131.)

17 Studwell, J., *The China Dream: The Quest for the Last Great Untapped Market on Earth*, Profile Books, 2002, p. 19.

## 2 The political and economic context

1 Of the estimated 23m migrant workers who failed to return from the countryside to the cities after their traditional annual Chinese New Year holiday in February 2009, only 30% or roughly 7m are believed to have subsequently returned to their jobs. Many were the victims of the global crisis, but others were laid off by companies that had been forced out of business by rising product quality standards in the wake of a series of product and food safety scandals, or by rising labour and land costs in southern China. Yet a sizeable proportion simply decided that frozen wages in coastal provinces were not significantly higher than rural incomes, which continue to rise with support from central government.

2 The concept of "harmonious society" (*hexie shehui*) was launched at the CCP Central Committee's Fourth Plenum in late 2004 and was developed further following the Central Committee's Sixth Plenum in late 2006.

3 The 2007 National Bureau of Statistics Household Survey was cited by the World Bank to show that the number of absolute poor (those earning less than $1 a day) fell from 250m in 1978 to 34m in 1999; but more significantly, the number had already fallen to 96m by 1988.

4 Liu Shaoqi was chairman of the PRC from 1959 to 1968. He was a moderate who opposed Mao's collectivisation policies in the 1950s and gained political ground after the failed Great Leap Forward. Perceived

as a threat to Mao's power, Liu was labelled a "capitalist-roader" and traitor in the Cultural Revolution. He was tortured and died through lack of medical treatment in 1969. In 1980 Liu was posthumously rehabilitated and given a state funeral.

5 The North Korean equivalent, *juche*, remains a central tenet of government policy in the Democratic People's Republic of Korea. See French, P., *North Korea: The Paranoid Peninsula – A Modern History*, Zed Books, 2005.

6 The creation of people's communes (*renmin gongshe*) at the start of the Great Leap Forward were a core part of Mao's dream to overtake steel production (the building blocks of an industrial economy) in the United States and the UK within the space of a few years. Communes, of which some 26,000 (comprising 99% of the peasant population) were established, formed the largest collective units, ranging from 4,000 to as many as 20,000 households. Within the communes, brigades and production teams split community work – everything from ploughing and construction to child care and cooking.

7 Mao's decision to go it alone was no doubt influenced by his falling out with Nikita Khrushchev, who had come to power in the Soviet Union after Stalin's death in 1954 and who subsequently discredited Stalin (Mao's old ally), notably in his Secret speech at the 20th Congress in 1956, highlighting the failure of Stalin's agricultural policies – including collectivisation – in the Soviet Union.

8 The Great Leap Forward marked an attempt by Mao to turn China into a modern industrialised economy in the space of a few short years. Workers in backyard furnaces melted down every available scrap of metal to create pig iron that was unusable for any practical purpose. Meanwhile, agricultural production, for which insane claims had been made by competing local officials, was hit by a double whammy of poor weather and the disincentives of communisation. The result was a catastrophic famine. The official toll of famine-related deaths recorded in China for the years during the Great Leap Forward is 14m, though unofficial estimates range from 20m to 43m. (For a definitive account, see Becker, J., *Hungry Ghosts: Mao's Secret Famine*, The Free Press, 1997.) With his policies discredited, Mao lost political ground to moderates under Liu Shaoqi, who became chairman in 1959 and reintroduced economic reconstruction measures, which included limited market reforms such as financial incentives for farmers and workers to raise production levels. Mao would eventually regain the political initiative by mobilising students in what became the Cultural

Revolution (1966–76), dislodging Liu, who was tortured by Red Guards and died in prison in 1969.

9 Huang Yasheng, *Capitalism with Chinese Characteristics*, Cambridge University Press, 2008, p. 227.

10 The renminbi is currently linked to a basket of currencies, including the US dollar, euro, Japanese yen, South Korean won and others. Since 2007 it has been limited to a maximum daily fluctuation of no more than 0.5%.

## 3 Assessing the market: pre-market entry

1 From the 1930s until 1949, Shanghai was China's largest and most dynamic commercial centre and a base for international investment, manufacturing and trade. Shunned by the Beijing leadership for 40 years, Shanghai finally came in from the cold with the creation of Pudong New Area in 1990 and the city's heightened profile in central government through the efforts of President Jiang Zemin, a former CCP secretary-general there.

2 Ma, D. and Summers, T., *Is China's Growth Moving Inland?*, Chatham House Asia-Pacific Position Paper, October 2009.

3 The Three Gorges Dam was a controversial project pushed through by former Premier Li Peng (a native of Sichuan province, born in the capital Chengdu and closely linked to the city of Yibin, near the dam). One of the largest hydropower projects in the world, the Three Gorges Dam has been criticised by environmentalists for ......

4 Still in use today, the Grand Canal is believed to be the longest canal in the world, running 1,114 miles from Hangzhou to Beijing. The earliest sections date back to 5BC, though the various sections were not combined until the Sui dynasty (581–618AD).

## 5 Setting up: corporate structures and tax issues

1 Glenny, M., *McMafia: Seriously Organised Crime*, Vintage Books, 2009, p. 365. The phrase means that provincial officials can carry on being corrupt as long as they don't get caught by the central authorities. During his Southern Tour in 1992, Deng Xiaoping was quoted as saying: "It doesn't matter whether the cat is black or white, as long as it catches mice." This signalled the resumption of market-focused economic policy in China after the post-Tiananmen freeze on reform.

2 Economist Intelligence Unit, *China Hand*, 2009, Chapter 4 Investing. Specific steps required are as follows:
   1. Initial contact with local officials. This can be made either through a

Chinese "sponsor" (often a local chamber of commerce or law firm) or directly by the foreign company.

2. Feasibility study. This is prepared by the foreign investor and is the same as a joint-venture feasibility study.

3. Formal application. The feasibility study is submitted to the investment approval authority, along with an application and the proposed articles of association. Testimonials and documents on the financial credit of the foreign investor must also be submitted. A decision on the application should normally be handed down within 90 days.

4. Written reply from the local government. The reply must be presented in writing by the local government from the county level upward of the area where the foreign investor wants to be established.

5. Import list. This will comprise a list of items to be imported.

6. Registration. The WOFE should register with the local office of the SAIC within 30 days of approval for a business licence. The company must then register with the tax bureau, customs office and SAFE within 30 days of receiving the licence.

7. Certificate of incorporation of the applicant company and certificate of current status or proof of identity for individual investors which must be notarised and then authenticated by the applicable Chinese embassy or consulate.

8. Premises notarised. In some of the big cities WOFEs are now required to have their premises notarised.

3 Before the law came into effect on January 1st 2008, the central government estimated that foreign firms would pay Rmb41 billion ($6 billion) a year more in taxes while domestic firms would pay Rmb134 billion ($20 billion).

## 6 Making acquisitions work

1 According to *China Hand* (Chapter 4), op. cit., regulators look at the following:

- where the merger or acquisition would lead to a company controlling 25% or more of the Chinese market;
- where the foreign investor already controls 20% of the Chinese market;
- where the foreign investor has assets in China of more than Rmb3 billion ($441m);
- where the foreign investor has annual sales in China exceeding Rmb1.5 billion ($220m).

2 A toxic chemical typically used in the paint industry, melamine also

appears to raise the protein level of milk. This property was used to artificially raise protein levels in milk (all of which is produced from powdered milk and water in China) to the required level set by the government.

## 7 Human resources: attracting and retaining talent

1 Clean technology or cleantech includes renewable energy (solar power, wind power, hydropower, biofuels and biomass), environmentally friendly transport, electric motors and other appliances that are more energy-efficient (such as lighting). Cleantech aims to create electricity and fuels with as light an environmental footprint as possible.

2 For updated information on compensation and benefits for both international and local staff, refer to surveys published by international HR recruitment companies which are active in the mainland market: Korn-Ferry; Spencer Stuart; Heidrick & Struggles; A.T. Kearney; Watson Wyatt; MRI; SRHM-Mercer; Hewitt Associates; Hudson.

## 8 Dealing with corruption and financial crime

1 The Discipline Inspection Committee, Supervisory Office and Marxism-Leninism Research Office of Beijing University, eds, *Fanfubai Zongheng Tan* (Essays on Combating Corruption), Beijing University Press, 1994. Other Chinese definitions are narrower: Wang Huning calls it the "abuse of the public office" in *Fan fubai: Zhongguo de Shiyan* (Combating Corruption: the Chinese Experiment), Beijing Sanhuan Press, 1993.

2 www.transparency.org/news_room/in_focus/2008/cpi2008/cpi_2008_ table. The composite index incorporates perceptions of the level of official graft by businesspeople and analysts.

3 Sun Yan, *Corruption and Market in Contemporary China*, Cornell University Press, 2004, page 4.

## 10 Future China

1 Huang Yasheng, op. cit.

2 China Daily Industry Updates, "Multinationals rev up R&D presence in China", December 26th 2008.

3 Kynge, J., *China Shakes the World: The Rise of a Hungry Nation*, Weidenfeld & Nicolson, 2006.

4 Zhang Dian, Jim Chiyung, Liu Chusheng: "Climate change, social unrest and dynastic transition in ancient China", *Chinese Science Bulletin* 50, 2, 2005, p. 137.

# APPENDICES

# 1 Facts and figures

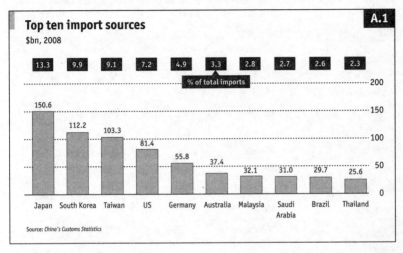

**Top ten import sources**
$bn, 2008

A.1

% of total imports

| 13.3 | 9.9 | 9.1 | 7.2 | 4.9 | 3.3 | 2.8 | 2.7 | 2.6 | 2.3 |

150.6 · 112.2 · 103.3 · 81.4 · 55.8 · 37.4 · 32.1 · 31.0 · 29.7 · 25.6

Japan · South Korea · Taiwan · US · Germany · Australia · Malaysia · Saudi Arabia · Brazil · Thailand

Source: *China's Customs Statistics*

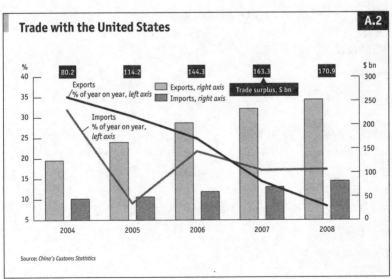

**Trade with the United States**

A.2

Exports, *right axis*
Imports, *right axis*
Trade surplus, $ bn

Exports
% of year on year, *left axis*

Imports
% of year on year, *left axis*

| 80.2 | 114.2 | 144.3 | 163.3 | 170.9 |

2004 · 2005 · 2006 · 2007 · 2008

Source: *China's Customs Statistics*

## Table A.1 **Sources of utilised FDI, 2008**

| Country/region | Utilised FDI ($m) | % share | Projects (no.) | % share |
|---|---|---|---|---|
| Hong Kong | 41,036.40 | 44.41 | 12,857 | 46.73 |
| British Virgin Islands | 15,953.84 | 17.27 | 975 | 3.54 |
| Singapore | 4,435.29 | 4.8 | 757 | 2.75 |
| Japan | 3,652.35 | 3.95 | 1,438 | 5.23 |
| Cayman Islands | 3,144.97 | 3.40 | 216 | 0.79 |
| South Korea | 3,135.32 | 3.39 | 2,226 | 8.09 |
| United States | 2,944.34 | 3.19 | 1,772 | 6.44 |
| Taiwan | 1,898.68 | 2.05 | 2,360 | 8.58 |
| Mauritius | 1,493.71 | 1.62 | 133 | 0.48 |
| United Kingdom | 914.01 | 0.99 | 365 | 1.33 |
| Germany | 900.49 | 0.97 | 390 | 1.42 |
| Netherlands | 862.16 | 0.93 | 152 | 0.55 |
| France | 587.75 | 0.64 | 199 | 0.72 |
| Macau | 581.61 | 0.63 | 435 | 1.58 |
| Canada | 543.28 | 0.59 | 410 | 1.49 |
| Italy | 493.26 | 0.53 | 293 | 1.06 |
| Denmark | 293.76 | 0.32 | 49 | 0.18 |
| Malaysia | 246.96 | 0.27 | 219 | 0.80 |
| Spain | 208.90 | 0.23 | 127 | 0.46 |
| Ireland | 198.29 | 0.21 | 27 | 0.10 |
| Indonesia | 167.25 | 0.18 | 45 | 0.16 |
| Sweden | 139.17 | 0.15 | 78 | 0.28 |
| Luxembourg | 132.83 | 0.14 | 29 | 0.11 |
| Austria | 132.55 | 0.14 | 43 | 0.16 |
| Thailand | 129.21 | 0.14 | 56 | 0.20 |

Source: Ministry of Commerce

Table A.2 **Sources of FDI by sector, 2008**

| Sectors | Enterprises (no.) | % annual change | Amount ($bn) | % annual change |
|---|---|---|---|---|
| Agriculture, forestry, fishery, animal husbandry | 917 | −12.5 | 1.19 | 28.9 |
| Mining & quarrying | 149 | −36.3 | 0.57 | 17.0 |
| Manufacturing industry | 11,568 | −39.7 | 49.89 | 22.1 |
| Electricity, gas, water | 320 | −9.1 | 1.70 | 58.1 |
| Construction industry | 262 | −14.9 | 1.09 | 151.6 |
| Transport, storage, post & telecoms | 523 | −20.5 | 2.85 | 42.1 |
| Information technology | 1,286 | −7.6 | 2.77 | 86.8 |
| Wholesale & retail industry | 5,854 | −7.6 | 4.43 | 65.6 |
| Lodging & restaurant industry | 633 | −32.5 | 0.94 | −9.9 |
| Financial services | 25 | −51.0 | 0.57 | 122.5 |
| Property | 452 | −68.7 | 18.59 | 8.8 |
| Leasing, commercial services | 3,138 | −11.3 | 5.06 | 25.9 |
| Scientific research | 1,839 | 7.2 | 1.51 | 64.2 |
| Irrigation works, environment | 138 | −10.4 | 0.34 | 24.7 |
| Residential services | 205 | −24.1 | 0.57 | −21.1 |
| Education | 24 | 60.0 | 0.04 | 12.2 |
| Health, social security, welfare | 10 | −23.1 | 0.02 | 63.1 |
| Cultural, sports, entertainment | 170 | −17.9 | 0.26 | −42.8 |
| Total | 27,514 | −27.3 | 92.40 | 23.6 |

Source: Statistical Communique on the 2008 National Economic and Social Development

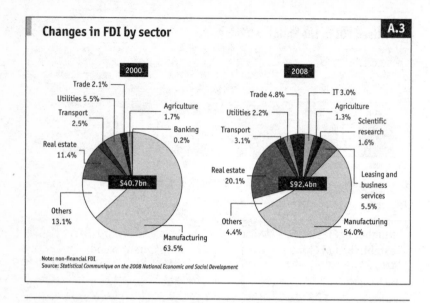

**Changes in FDI by sector** A.3

2000

Trade 2.1%
Utilities 5.5%
Transport 2.5%
Agriculture 1.7%
Banking 0.2%
Real estate 11.4%
$40.7bn
Others 13.1%
Manufacturing 63.5%

2008

Trade 4.8%
IT 3.0%
Utilities 2.2%
Agriculture 1.3%
Transport 3.1%
Scientific research 1.6%
Real estate 20.1%
$92.4bn
Leasing and business services 5.5%
Others 4.4%
Manufacturing 54.0%

Note: non-financial FDI
Source: *Statistical Communique on the 2008 National Economic and Social Development*

Table A.3 **Top ten foreign-invested enterprises in China, 2008**

| Rank | Company | Sales (Rmb bn) |
|------|---------|----------------|
| 1 | Hongfujin Precision Industry (Shenzhen) | 187.5 |
| 2 | Nokia Telecommunications | 95.7 |
| 3 | CNOOC China | 78.9 |
| 4 | Tech-Com (Shanghai) Computer | 73.2 |
| 5 | FAW-Volkswagen Sales Co | 72.4 |
| 6 | Tech-Front (Shanghai) Computer | 65.8 |
| 7 | Angang Steel | 65.5 |
| 8 | Shanghai General Motors | 65.1 |
| 9 | FAW-Volkswagen Automobile | 64.1 |
| 10 | Motorola (China) Electronics | 56.3 |

Source: Ministry of Commerce

## Utilised FDI in the Yangtze River Delta

A.4

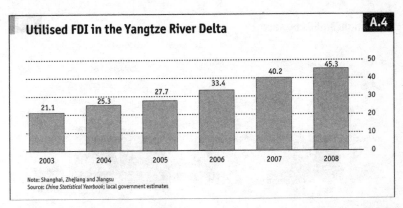

Values: 2003: 21.1; 2004: 25.3; 2005: 27.7; 2006: 33.4; 2007: 40.2; 2008: 45.3

Note: Shanghai, Zhejiang and Jiangsu
Source: *China Statistical Yearbook*; local government estimates

## Number of FIEs established in China

A.5

'000

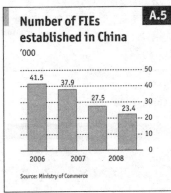

2006: 41.5; 2007: 37.9; 2008: 27.5, 23.4

Source: Ministry of Commerce

## China's outward direct investment trend

A.6

$bn

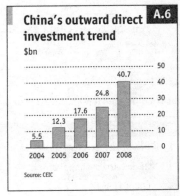

2004: 5.5; 2005: 12.3; 2006: 17.6; 2007: 24.8; 2008: 40.7

Source: CEIC

## China's foreign trade-balance cycles

A.7

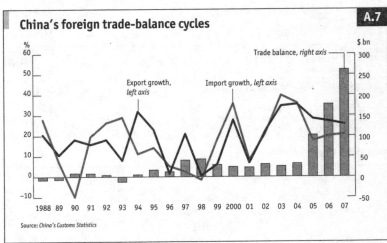

Trade balance, right axis
Export growth, left axis
Import growth, left axis

Source: *China's Customs Statistics*

185

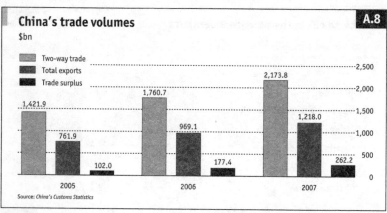

**China's trade volumes**
$bn

A.8

Source: *China's Customs Statistics*

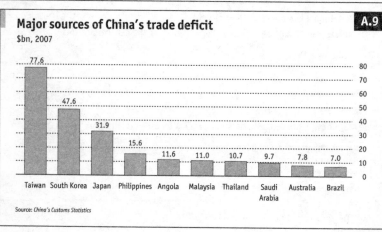

**Major sources of China's trade deficit**
$bn, 2007

A.9

Source: *China's Customs Statistics*

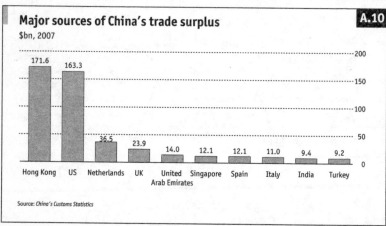

**Major sources of China's trade surplus**
$bn, 2007

A.10

Source: *China's Customs Statistics*

Table A.4 **China's top ten advertising agencies by revenue, Rmb m**

| Rank | Company | 2007 | 2008 |
|---|---|---|---|
| 1 | Focus Media (China) Holdings | 3,700 | 5,396 |
| 2 | White Horse Adshel | 967 | 1,102 |
| 3 | Beijing Dentsu Advertising | 792 | 982 |
| 4 | Jiangsu Dahe International Advertising | 608 | 852 |
| 5 | Saatchi & Saatchi Great Wall | 525 | 685 |
| 6 | AVIC Culture | 487 | 663 |
| 7 | Shanghai Lintas | 553 | 588 |
| 8 | Shanghai Shentong JCDecaux Metro Advertising | 126 | 408 |
| 9 | JCDecaux Momentum Shanghai Airport Advertising | 299 | 367 |
| 10 | Tulip Mega Media | 40 | 281 |

Source: China Advertising Association

Table A.5 **China's top ten advertising agencies by billings, Rmb m**

| Rank | Company | 2007 | 2008 |
|---|---|---|---|
| 1 | Focus Media | 3,700 | 5,396 |
| 2 | McCann Erickson-Guangming | 4,235 | 4,928 |
| 3 | Shanghai Leo Burnett | 4,299 | 4,756 |
| 4 | J. Walter Thomson (Shanghai) | 4,170 | 4,710 |
| 5 | Saatchi & Saatchi Great Wall | 4,314 | 4,278 |
| 6 | Beijing Dentsu Advertising | 3,435 | 3,569 |
| 7 | Beijing Weilai Advertising | 2,428 | 3,465 |
| 8 | DDB China (Shanghai) | 1,513 | 2,040 |
| 9 | Guangdong Carat Media Services (Shanghai) | 1,351 | 1,846 |
| 10 | Kinetic China | na | 1,577 |

Source: China Advertising Association

# 2 CCP politburo standing committee members, 2010

| | |
|---|---|
| Hu Jintao | President, CCP Secretary-General, CMC Chairman |
| Wu Bangguo | NPC Standing Committee Chairman |
| Wen Jiabao | Premier |
| Jia Qinglin | Chairman of the Chinese People's Political Consultative Conference |
| Xi Jinping | Vice-President, top-ranked member of CPC Secretariat |
| Li Keqiang | Executive Vice-Premier |
| Li Changchun | "Propaganda Chief" |
| He Guoqiang | Head of Central Commission for Discipline Inspection |
| Zhou Yongkang | Head of Political and Legislative Affairs Committee |

## Members of the Politburo of the CPC Central committee

| | |
|---|---|
| Wang Lequan | Luo Gan |
| Wang Zhaoguo | Zhou Yongkang |
| Hui Liangyu | Hu Jintao |
| Liu Qi | Yu Zhengsheng |
| Liu Yunshan | He Guoqiang |
| Li Changchun | Jia Qinglin |
| Wu Yi | Guo Boxiong |
| Wu Bangguo | Cao Gangchuan |
| Wu Guanzheng | Zeng Qinghong |
| Zhang Lichang | Zeng Peiyan |
| Zhang Dejiang | Wen Jiabao |

There will be a reshuffle in late 2012.

# 3  Glossary

| | |
|---|---|
| ABC | Agricultural Bank of China |
| AML | Anti-Money-laundering Law |
| BOC | Bank of China |
| CBRC | China Banking Regulatory Commission |
| CCB | China Construction Bank |
| CCDI | Central Commission for Discipline Inspection |
| CIRC | China Insurance Regulatory Commission |
| CIT | Corporate Income Tax law |
| CMC | Central Military Commission |
| CNOOC | China National Offshore Oil Corporation |
| CNPC | China National Petroleum Corporation |
| CPC | Communist Party of China |
| CPPCC | Chinese People's Political Consultative Conference |
| CSRC | China Securities Regulatory Commission |
| FIE | Foreign-invested enterprise |
| GAQSIQ | General Administration of Quality Supervision, Entry and Exit Inspection and Quarantine |
| GAPP | General Administration of Press & Publication |
| ICBC | Industrial & Commercial Bank of China |
| KMT | Kuomintang (Nationalist party) |
| MIIT | Ministry of Information Industry and Technology |
| Mofcom | Ministry of Commerce |
| MOF | Ministry of Finance |
| MOS | Ministry of Supervision |
| NBCP | National Bureau of Corruption Prevention |
| NDRC | National Development & Reform Commission |
| NPC | National People's Congress |
| PBOC | People's Bank of China |
| PLA | People's Liberation Army |
| PRC | People's Republic of China |
| PSB | Public Security Bureau |
| QBPC | Quality Brands Protection Committee |
| SAFE | State Administration of Foreign Exchange |
| SAIC | State Administration of Industry and Commerce |
| SARFT | State Administration for Radio, Film and Television |

| SASAC | State-owned Assets Supervision and Administration Commission |
| SAT | State Administration of Taxation |
| SEC | US Securities Exchange Commission |
| Sinopec | China Petroleum & Chemical Corporation |
| SOE | State-owned enterprise |
| WOFE | Wholly owned foreign enterprise |
| WTO | World Trade Organisation |

# 4 International law firms

China has more than 15,000 law firms and 166,000 lawyers – a tiny proportion of the total population. Dozens of international law firms operate on the mainland, specialising in areas such as M&A, arbitration, dispute resolution and IP protection. They include:

Allen & Overy
Allens Arthur Robinson
Baker & McKenzie
Barlow Lyde & Gilbert
Clifford Chance
Davis Wright Tremaine
Dechert
DLA Piper
Eversheds
Faegre & Benson
Freshfields Bruckhaus Deringer
Greenberg Traurig
Heller Ehrman
Herbert Smith
Kayer Scholer
Kirkland & Ellis
Linklaters

Lovells
Mallesons Stephen Jaques
Morrison & Foerster
Paul, Weiss, Rifkind, Wharton & Garrison
O'Melveny & Myers
Rouse & Co
Salans
Shearman & Sterling
Simmons & Simmons
Skadden, Arps, Slate, Meagher & Flom
Slaughter & May
Squire, Sanders & Dempsey
Troutman Sanders
White & Case

# 5  Recommended reading

## Business

Bremmer, I., *The J Curve: A New Way to Understand why Nations Rise and Fall*, Simon & Schuster, 2006.

Brown, K., *Friends and Enemies: China in the 21st Century*, Anthem Press, 2009.

Clissold, T., *Mr China: A Memoir*, Constable & Robinson, 2004.

Duckett, J., *The Chinese State's Retreat from Health: Policy and Politics of Retrenchment*, Routledge, 2010.

Fernandez, J.A. and Underwood, L., *China CEO: Voices of Experience from 20 International Business Leaders*, Wiley, 2006.

Huang, Y., *Capitalism with Chinese Characteristics*, Cambridge University Press, 2008

Kitto, M., *China Cuckoo*, Constable & Robinson, 2009.

Kynge, J., *China Shakes the World: The Rise of a Hungry Nation*, Weidenfeld & Nicolson, 2006.

Mann, J., *Beijing Jeep*, Westview Press, updated edn, 1997.

Midler, P., *Poorly Made in China: An Insider's Account of the Tactics Behind China's Production Game*, Wiley, 2009.

Pacek, N. and Thorniley, D., *Emerging Markets*, Profile Books, 2007.

Schaub, M., *China: The Art of Law*, Kluwer Law International, 2007.

Studwell, J., *The China Dream: The Elusive Quest for the Greatest Untapped Market on Earth*, 3rd edn, Profile Books, 2005.

## Politics

Bao, P., Chiang, R., Ignatius, A. and Dietz, N., *Prisoner of the State: the Secret Journal of Premier Zhao Ziyang*, Simon & Schuster, 2009.

Dittmar, L. and Lu, G., eds, *China's Deep Reform*, Rowman & Littlefield Publishers, 2006.

Nathan, A. and Gilley, B., *China's New Rulers: The Secret Files*, New York Review of Books, 2003.

Shambaugh, D., *China's Communist Party: Atrophy and Adaptation*, Woodrow Wilson Center Press & University of California Press, 2008.

## General

Crow, C., *400 Million Customers*, Harper & Brothers, 1937.

Bickers, R., *Empire Made Me: An Englishman Adrift in Shanghai*, Columbia University Press, 2003.

Elvin, M., *The Retreat of the Elephants: An Environmental History of China*, Yale University Press, 2004.

Fleming, P., *News from Tartary*, Alden Press, 1936.

French, P., *Through the Looking Glass: China's Foreign Journalists from Opium Wars to Mao*, Hong Kong University Press, 2009.

Hessler, P., *River Town: Two Years on the Yangtze*, HarperCollins, 2001.

Hessler, P., *Oracle Bones: A Journey Between China's Past and Present*, HarperCollins, 2006.

Hewitt, D., *Getting Rich First: Life in a Changing China*, Chatto & Windus, 2007.

Hopkirk, P., *Trespassers on the Roof of the World: The Secret Exploration of Tibet*, John Murray, 1982.

Jenner, W., *The Tyranny of History*, Viking Adult, 1992.

Larmer, B., *Operation Yao Ming: The Chinese Sports Empire, American Big Business, and the Making of an NBA Superstar*, Penguin Books, 2005.

Leys, S., *Chinese Shadows*, Viking Adult, 1997.

Macleod, C. and Zhang, L., *China Remembers*, Oxford University Press, 1999.

Pomfret, J., *Chinese Lessons: Five Classmates and the Story of the New China*, Henry Holt and Company, 2006.

Seth, V., *From Heaven Lake: Travels through Sinkiang and Tibet*, Chatto & Windus, 1983.

Spence, J., *The Search for Modern China*, W.W. Norton, 1990.

Timberlake, P., *The Story of the Icebreakers in China*, The 48 Group Club, 1994.

## Periodicals, blogs and newsletters

Access Asia www.accessasia.co.uk
China Economic Quarterly www.dragonomics.net
Caixin http://english/caing.com
China Law Blog www.chinalawblog.com
Danwei.org www.danwei.org

# Index

## X
Xbox 65
Xi, Jinping 29-30
*xiagang* (outplacement) 135-6
Xinhua news agency 32, 147
Xizang (Tibet) 25-6, 32, 168
Xugong Group Construction
    Machinery 96

## Y
Yangtze River Delta (YRD) 58,
    60-1, 185
Yaohan, Japan 13

YRC Worldwide 82
YRD *see* Yangtze River Delta
Yum! 17

## Z
Zhang, Wenzhong 149
Zhao, Ziyang 29, 39
Zheshang Bank 45
Zhou, Enlai 39, 50
Zinnov Management Consultants
    163
zones *see* investment zones
Zong, Qinghou 14